Fishamble: The New Play Company presents

T0346851

DUCK
DUCK
GOOSE

by Caitríona Daly

Duck Duck Goose opened as part of the Dublin Theatre Festival at Pavilion Theatre on 1 October 2021 and, with the support of the Arts Council, toured to Draíocht, Everyman Theatre, Watergate Theatre, Lyric Theatre, and Belltable. It was developed as part of *A Play for Ireland*, a two-year artist development initiative in 2018/19, to mark Fishamble's 30th year, in association with Pavilion Theatre, Draíocht, Lime Tree & Belltable, Everyman Theatre, Town Hall Theatre, and Lyric Theatre.

Cast

Leo	John Doran
Andy	Naoise Dunbar
Jane	Caitríona Ennis
Davey	Liam Heslin
Chris	Aidan Moriarty
Sarah	Roseanna Purcell

Production Team

Director	Jim Culleton
Producer	Eva Scanlan
Set and Lighting Designer	Paul Keogan
Composer & Sound Designer	Carl Kennedy
Costume Designer	Saileóg O'Halloran
Associate Costume Designer	Eimear Farrell
Movement Director	Bryan Burroughs
Dialect Coach	Cathal Quinn
Production Manager	Marie Tierney
Stage Manager	Steph Ryan
Assistant Stage Manager	Sarah Purcell
Line Producer	Cally Shine
Stage Carpenter	Jason Coogans
Chief LX	Joe Glasgow
Set Builder	Ian Thompson
Dramaturg	Gavin Kostick
Production Coordinator	Ronan Carey
Marketing	Chandrika Narayanan-Mohan & Freya Gillespie
PR	O'Doherty Communications
Filmed by	Media Coop
Graphic Design	Publicis Dublin
Poster Image	Leo Byrne
Legal Advisor	Deirdre Flannery

The production runs for approximately 80 minutes, with no interval.

An education pack to accompany this production is available for teachers on request. Please contact **info@fishamble.com** for details.

About Fishamble

Fishamble is an Irish theatre company that discovers, develops and produces new plays of national importance with a global reach. It has toured its productions to audiences throughout Ireland, and to 19 other countries. It champions the role of the playwright, typically supporting over 50% of the writers of all new plays produced on the island of Ireland each year. Fishamble has received many awards in Ireland and internationally, including an Olivier Award.

'the much-loved Fishamble [is] a global brand with international theatrical presence... an unswerving force for new writing
Irish Times

'Ireland's leading new writing company' **The Stage**

'the respected Dublin company...forward-thinking Fishamble'
New York Times

'excellent Fishamble...Ireland's terrific Fishamble' **Guardian**

'when Fishamble is [in New York], you've got to go'
Time Out New York

'that great Irish new writing company, Fishamble'
Lyn Gardner, Stage Door

'Fishamble puts electricity into the National Grid of dreams'
Sebastian Barry

Fishamble Staff: Jim Culleton (Artistic Director), Eva Scanlan (General Manager & Producer), Gavin Kostick (Literary Manager), Chandrika Narayanan-Mohan (Marketing and Fundraising Manager), Ronan Carey (Office and Production Coordinator), Freya Gillespie (Development & Marketing Officer), Cally Shine (Line Producer)

Fishamble Board: Peter Finnegan, John McGrane, Louise Molloy, Doireann Ní Bhriain (Chair), Ronan Nulty, John O'Donnell, Siobhan O'Leary (Vice Chair), Colleen Savage

Fishamble is funded by the Arts Council, Dublin City Council, and Culture Ireland.

Comhairle Cathrach
Bhaile Átha Cliath
Dublin City Council

Cultúr Éireann
Culture Ireland

Fishamble's recent and current productions include

- *On Blueberry Hill* by Sebastian Barry (since 2017) touring in Ireland, Europe, Off-Broadway, West End, and online

- *Before* by Pat Kinevane (since 2018) touring in Ireland, internationally, and online, as well as a bilingual version *Before/Sula*

- *Mustard* by Eva O'Connor (since 2020) on tour in Ireland, internationally, and online

- *On the Horizon* in association with Dirty Protest, by Shannon Yee, Hefin Robinson, Michael Patrick, Oisín Kearney, Samantha O'Rourke, Ciara Elizabeth Smyth, Connor Allen (2021) online

- *Tiny Plays for a Brighter Future* by Niall Murphy, Signe Lury, Eva-Jane Gaffney (2021) online

- *Tiny Plays 24/7* by Lora Hartin, Maria Popovic, Ciara Elizabeth Smyth, Caitríona Daly, Conor Hanratty, Julia Marks, Patrick O'Laoghaire, Eric O'Brien, Grace Lobo, Ryan Murphy (2020) online

- *The Alternative* by Oisín Kearney and Michael Patrick (2019) on tour to Pavilion Theatre, Draíocht, Belltable, Everyman Theatre, Town Hall Theatre, and Lyric Theatre

- *Haughey | Gregory* by Colin Murphy (2018–19) in the Abbey Theatre, Mountjoy Prison, Dáil Éireann, Croke Park, and Larkin Community College, as well as on national tour

- *The Humours of Bandon* by Margaret McAuliffe (2017–19) touring in Ireland, UK, US, and Australia

- *Rathmines Road* by Deirdre Kinahan (2018) in coproduction with the Abbey Theatre

- *Drip Feed* by Karen Cogan (2018) in coproduction with Soho Theatre, touring in Ireland and UK

- *GPO 1818* by Colin Murphy (2018) to mark the bicentenary of the GPO

- *Maz & Bricks* by Eva O'Connor (2017–18) on national and international tour

- *Forgotten, Silent and Underneath* by Pat Kinevane (since 2007, 2011 and 2014, respectively) touring in Ireland, UK, Europe, US, Australia, New Zealand, and online

- *Charolais* by Noni Stapleton (2017) in New York

- *Inside the GPO* by Colin Murphy (2016) performed in the GPO during Easter

- *Tiny Plays for Ireland and America* by 26 writers (2016) at the Kennedy Center, Washington DC, and Irish Arts Center, New York, as part of Ireland 100

- *Mainstream* by Rosaleen McDonagh (2016) in coproduction with Project Arts Centre

- *Invitation to a Journey* by David Bolger, Deirdre Gribbin and Gavin Kostick (2016) in coproduction with CoisCeim, Crash Ensemble and Galway International Arts Festival

- *Little Thing, Big Thing* by Donal O'Kelly (2014–16) touring in Ireland, UK, Europe, US and Australia

- *Swing* by Steve Blount, Peter Daly, Gavin Kostick and Janet Moran (2014–16) touring in Ireland, UK, Europe, US, Australia and New Zealand

- *Spinning* by Deirdre Kinahan (2014) at Dublin Theatre Festival

- *The Wheelchair on My Face* by Sonya Kelly (2013–14) touring in Ireland, UK, Europe and US.

Fishamble wishes to thank the following Friends of Fishamble & Corporate Members for their invaluable support:

Alan & Rosemary Ashe, ATM Accounting Services, Mary Banotti, Tania Banotti, Doireann Ní Bhriain, Colette and Barry Breen, Sean Brett, John Butler, Elizabeth Carroll, Sandra Carroll, Breda Cashe, Barry Cassidy, Maura Connolly, Molissa Fenley, John & Yvonne Healy, Alison Howard, Gillie and Ross Hinds, Stephen Lambert, Angus Laverty, Patrick Lonergan, Sheelagh Malin, John McGrane, Monica McInerney, Ger McNaughton, Anne McQuillan, Louise Molloy, Sinead Moriarty, Liz Morrin, Pat Moylan, Dympna Murray, Liz Nugent, Lisney, Siobhan O'Beirne, Tom O'Connor Consultant, Siobhan O'Leary, Muiris O'Reilly, Andrew and Delyth Parkes, Margaret Rogers, David & Veronica Rowe, Judy Regan, Jennifer Russell, Eileen Ryan, Colleen Savage, William Smith, Mary Stephenson, and Joan Westrap. Thank you also to all those who do not wish to be credited.

fishamble.com   facebook.com/fishamble   twitter.com/fishamble

Fishamble is funded by The Arts Council and Dublin City Council. Its international touring is supported by Culture Ireland.

Acknowledgements

Thanks to the following for their help with this production: Rachel West, Liz Meaney, Elaine Connolly, Hannah Gordis, and all at the Arts Council; Ray Yeates, Sinéad Connolly, and all at Dublin City Council Arts Office; Christine Sisk, Ciaran Walsh, Valerie Behan, and all at Culture Ireland; Willie White, and everyone at Dublin Theatre Festival; Louise Donlon, and all at Lime Tree Theatre/ Belltable; Jimmy Fay, Rebecca Mairs, and all at the Lyric Theatre; Emer McGowan, and all at Draíocht; Hugh Murray, Niall O'Connell, and all at Pavilion Theatre; Sophie Motley, and all at The Everyman; Ruth Little; Joanna Cunningham, and all at the Watergate Theatre; Laura MacNaughton, Aoife McCollum and all at the O'Reilly Theatre; all at 3 Great Denmark Street; Deirdre Flannery, Andrea Martin, Liz Fitzgibbon, Eanna Hardwicke, Kevin Olohan, Emmet Byrne, Clare Dunne, Fionntán Larney, Karen McCartney, Oisín O'Donoghue, Daniel Culleton, Emma Finegan, Ronan Nulty, James Kelleher, Karen Muckian, and all at Publicis Dublin; Leo Byrne; Dr. Charlotte McIvor; Joy-Tendai Kangere; Professor Lousie Crowley; all at Smashing Times; all at Dublin Arts and Human Rights Festival; all those who have helped since this publication went to print.

Biographies

Caitríona Daly is a writer from Dublin. Her plays include *Panned*, *Test Dummy* (Irish Times Theatre Award Best New Play Nominee 2016) and *Normal* (Dublin Fringe 2017: Fishamble New Writing Award Nominee and First Fortnight Nominee). She was a participant in Six in the Attic, an Irish Theatre Institute initiative, from 2018–2019 and a participant on the inaugural Abbey Works programme in 2019. She is currently under commission with The Abbey Theatre and Fishamble: The New Play Company.

Jim Culleton is the artistic director of Fishamble: The New Play Company, for which he has directed productions on tour throughout Ireland, UK, Europe, Australia, New Zealand, Canada and the US, as well as online. His productions for Fishamble have won many Irish and international awards, including Olivier, The Stage, Scotsman Fringe First, and Irish Times Best Director Awards. Jim has also directed for Audible, the Abbey, the Gaiety, the Belgrade, 7:84 Scotland, Project, Amharclann de hÍde, Tinderbox, The Passion Machine, the Ark, Second Age, Dundee Rep, Draíocht, CoisCéim/Crash Ensemble/GIAF, RTÉ Radio 1, Frontline Defenders, Amnesty International, Little Museum of Dublin, Fighting Words, RTÉ lyric fm, Soho Theatre, Scripts Festival, Baptiste Programme, Vessel and APA (Australia), TNL (Canada), Solas Nua and Kennedy Center (Washington DC), Odyssey (LA), Origin, Irish Arts Center and 59E59 (Off-Broadway), as well as for Trafalgar Theatre Productions on the West End, and IAC/Symphony Space on Broadway. Jim has taught for NYU, NUI, GSA, Uversity, the Lir, Villanova, Notre Dame, JNU, UM, UMD, and TCD.

Eva Scanlan's current, upcoming, and recent producing work includes *Duck Duck Goose* by Caitríona Daly and *The Alternative* by Michael Patrick and Oisín Kearney, both at the Dublin Theatre Festival and on Irish tours; *The Treaty* by Colin Murphy at the National Concert Hall; *On Blueberry Hill* by Sebastian Barry on the West End, Off-Broadway, at the Dublin Theatre Festival and on Irish tour; *Rathmines Road* by Deirdre Kinahan at the Dublin Theatre Festival; *Before, Silent, Underneath*, and *Forgotten*, all by Pat Kinevane on tour in Ireland and internationally; *The Humours of Bandon* by Margaret McAuliffe; *Maz and Bricks* by Eva O'Connor; *Inside the GPO* by Colin Murphy; *Tiny Plays for Ireland and America* at the Kennedy Centre in Washington DC and the Irish Arts Centre in New York, and *Swing* by Steve Blount, Peter Daly, Gavin Kostick and Janet Moran on tour in Ireland, the UK, and Australia. Eva produces *The 24 Hour Plays: Dublin* at the Abbey Theatre in Ireland (2012–present), in association with the 24 Hour Play Company, New York, and has worked on *The 24 Hour Plays* on Broadway and *The 24 Hour Musicals* at the Gramercy Theatre. Previously, she was Producer of terraNOVA Collective in New York (2012–2015), where she produced *terraNOVA Rx: Four Plays in Rep* at IRT Theater, the soloNOVA Arts Festival, the Groundworks New Play Series, *Woman of Leisure* and *Panic* (FringeNYC), *P.S. Jones and the Frozen City*, among other projects.

John Doran will next appear in *The Teddybear's Picnic* directed by Louis Lovett for Theatre Lovett. Earlier this year he performed in *Goodnight Egg*, co-created by John, Ursula McGinn and Mollie Molumby. *Goodnight Egg* is a joyful new play with puppetry, miniatures and music, developed with support from The Arts Council's Project Award. In 2020 he played the role of Finbarr Lowe opposite Caitríona Ennis in *The Fall of the Second Republic* by Michael West, directed by Annie Ryan for the Corn Exchange on the Abbey Theatre stage. His further stage credits include *GYM / SWIM / PARTY* directed by Louise Lowe for Dublin Theatre Festival 2019.

Naoise Dunbar graduated from The Lir Academy in 2020. Recent credits include: *The Great Hunger*, *Fourteen Voices From The Bloodied Field* (Understudy) for The Abbey Theatre, Wexford Playwrights Studio Readings for the Wexford Arts Centre.

Caitríona Ennis' recent theatre work includes *A Christmas Carol* (The Gate Theatre); *Country Girls* (The Abbey Theatre's touring production); *Cuckoo* (Soho Theatre, London); *Ulysses* (Abbey Theatre); *Porcelain* (Peacock Theatre/Abbey Theatre); *A Holy Show* (Peacock Theatre); *Dublin by Lamplight* (Corn Exchange/Abbey Theatre); *Test Dummy* (nominated for Best Actress in the Irish Times Theatre Awards 2016, WeGetHighOnThis in association with Theatre Upstairs); *The Table* (Performance Corporation in association with Boca Del Lupo, Magnetic North Festival in Vancouver); *Wild Sky* (Irish Arts Centre New York, and an Irish national tour); *Scuttlers* (Royal Exchange Theatre, Manchester); *Spinning* (nominated for Best Supporting Actress in the Irish Times Theatre Awards 2015, Fishamble: The New Play Company); *Sluts* (Edinburgh Fringe 2011); *The Lark* (Smock Alley Theatre); *Narf* (Smock Alley Theatre); *Annabelle Star* (The Ark); *A Whistle in the Dark* (winner ISDA Award for Best Actress 2011); *A Couple of Poor Polish Speaking Romanians* (nominated for Best Actress, ISDA 2010). Caitriona has performed with ANU Productions, directed by Louise Lowe in *The State Commemoration*, *Taking to the Bed*, *The Boys of Foley Street* (nominated for Best Actress in the Irish Times Theatre Awards 2012); *Thirteen* (nominated for Best Actress at the Dublin Fringe Awards 2013); and *Angel Meadow* (winner of MTA Best Overall Production and Best Ensemble, HOME Manchester).

Liam Heslin trained at The Lir Academy. Theatre credits include: *The Seagull* (Druid); *14 Voices from the Bloodied Field* (Abbey Theatre); *DruidGregory* (Druid); *On the Outside* (Druid); *Asking For It* (Landmark Productions); *A Skull in Connemara* (Oldham Coliseum); *Zero Hour* (ANU); *The Lost O' Casey* (Abbey Theatre/ANU); *The Shaughraun* (Smock Alley Theatre); *The Plough and the Stars* (Lyric Hammersmith/ Gaiety Theatre); *The Good Father* (Rise Productions); *The Plough and the Stars* (Abbey Theatre); *On Corporation Street* (ANU/Home Manchester); *King Lear* (Second Age Theatre Company); *East of Berlin* (Brinkmanship/Project Arts Centre); *A Boy Called Nedd* (Bitter Like a Lemon/Theatre Upstairs); *Pals: The Irish at Gallipoli* (ANU); *Borstal Boy* (Verdant Productions); *The Clearing*, *Into the Woods*, *The Night Season*, *Mary Stuart*, *Scenes from the Big Picture*, *Poor Little Boy With No Arms*, *The Rover*, *The Suppliants*, *Love's Labour's Lost* (Lir Academy). Film and television credits include: *Dublin Oldschool*, *The Island of Evenings*, *Kaleidoscope*, *Fair City*.

Aidan Moriarty is a graduate of The Lir Academy in Dublin. Since graduating, he has worked on developments of *What The Telly Saw* and *The Tempest*, both directed by Lynne Parker. Whilst at The Lir, Aidan performed in productions of *Blood Wedding* (Dir. Caitriona McLaughlin); *The Merchant of Venice* (Dir. Lynne Parker) *Anatomy of a Suicide* (Dir. Tom Creed) and *The Comedy of Errors* (Dir. Mikel Murfi). He also performed in *Hostel 16* (Dir. Raymond Keane) at the Dublin Fringe Festival in 2016.

Roseanna Purcell's theatre credits include: *A Holy Show* (Verdant Productions); *My Romantic History* (Verdant Productions); *Midsummer* (Project Arts Centre); *Copper Face Jacks: The Musical* (Olympia Theatre); *Test Copy* (Self Penned, Nenagh Arts Centre); *Signatories* (Verdant Productions); *The Bridge Below The Town* (Livin' Dred); *Beyond The Brooklyn Sky* (Red Kettle); *AnnaBellaEema* (Rough Magic); *Birdy* (Peacock Theatre, Dublin Fringe Best Ensemble Award); *War of Attrition* (Devious Theatre, Dublin Fringe Best Female Performer nomination) and *Perfidia* (Theatre Upstairs). Film and television credits include: *Don't Go Where I Can't Find You* (Samson Films); *Joan Verra* (JV Productions/Blinder Films); *Fair City* (RTÉ); *Red Rock* (Virgin Media 1/BBC); *Take Me Swimming* (Feenish Productions) and *Nobody's Perfect* (BigO Media). Roseanna is currently developing her second play *Muck* following a work-in-development performance with Axis Theatre as part of the First Fortnight Festival 2021. She is also under commission from The Source Arts Centre via an Arts Council commission award. Roseanna is a graduate of The Gaiety School of Acting and University College Cork.

Paul Keogan's theatre credits include: *Tiny Plays for Ireland*, *Strandline* and *True Believers* (Fishamble, Dublin); *The Visiting Hour*, *The Snapper*, *Hamlet* (Gate Theatre, Dublin); *Sadie*, *Shirley Valentine*, *Double Cross*, (Lyric Theatre, Belfast); *Happy Days*, *Blood in the Dirt*, *Postcards from The Ledge*, *The Walworth Farce* (Landmark, Dublin); *Walls and Windows*, *The Great Hunger*, *Last Orders at the Dockside*, *Citysong*, *On Raftery's Hill* (Abbey Theatre, Dublin); *Love, Love, Love* (Lyric Hammersmith); *I Think We Are Alone* (Frantic Assembly, UK tour); *Lady Windermere's Fan* (Classic Spring, London); *A Streetcar Named Desire*, *Twelfth Night* and *The Hudsucker Proxy* (Liverpool Everyman & Playhouse); *Cyprus Avenue* (Abbey Theatre/Royal Court/Public Theater, NYC); *Harvest* (Royal Court); *The Caretaker* (Bristol Old Vic); *Incantata*, *Trad*, *The Matchbox* (Galway International); *Far Away*, *Sacrifice at Easter* (Corcadorca, Cork); *The Gaul* (Hull Truck Theatre); *Blue/Orange*, *Tribes* (Crucible, Sheffield); *Novecento* (Trafalgar Studios, London). Opera and Dance: *20 Shots of Opera* (Irish National Opera Film); *Elektra* and *The Marriage of Figaro* (Irish National Opera); *The Return of Ulysses* (Opera Collective, Ireland); *Falstaff* (Vienna Staatsoper); *Dialogues des Carmelites* (Grange Park Opera UK); *Powder Her Face* (Teatro Arriaga, Bilbao); *The Fairy Queen* (RIAM Dublin); *Maria de Buenos Aires* (Cork Opera House); *Wake* (Nationale Reisopera, Netherlands); *Lost* (Ballet Ireland); *Sama* & *Flight* (Rambert, London); *No Man's Land* (English National Ballet); *Cassandra*, *Hansel and Gretel* (Royal Ballet, London).

Carl Kennedy trained at Academy of Sound in Dublin. He has worked on numerous theatre productions, working with venues and companies including Fishamble: The New Play Company, The Abbey, The Gaiety, Rough Magic, Landmark, Decadent, The Lyric Theatre, Theatre Lovett, ANU Productions, HOME Manchester, Prime Cut Productions, HotForTheatre, Speckintime, Guna Nua, Loose Cannon, Peer to Peer, Siren, Broken Crow, Randolf SD and Theatre Makers. He has been nominated three times for the Irish Times Theatre Award for Best Sound Design. He also composes music and sound design for radio, TV and video games.

Saileóg O'Halloran's theatre credits include: *The Secret Space* (ANU Productions); *To The Lighthouse* (Cork Everyman & Hatch Productions); *The Great Hunger* (Abbey Theatre); *The Fall of the Second Republic* (Abbey Theatre/Corn Exchange); *Danse Macabre* (Macnas 2019); *Beckett's Room* (Dead Centre); *The Alternative* (Fishamble); *The Bluffers Guide to Suburbia* (Cork Midsummer & DTF 2019); *The Anvil* (ANU & Manchester International Festival); *The Misfits* (Corn Exchange); *Trial of the Century's* (Dublin Fringe 2018); *Macnas 2018, Copperface Jacks the Musical* (Verdant); *GPO1818* (Fishamble); *The Half of It* (MOMMO); *The Shitstorm* (Dublin Fringe); *The Seagull* (Corn Exchange); *To Hell In A Handbag* (Show In A Bag/Tiger Dublin Fringe); *Town is Dead* (Peacock Theatre); *Embodied* (Dublin Dance Festival); *Shibboleth* (Peacock Theatre); *Chekhov's First Play* (Dead Centre); *Thirteen* (Irish Times Judges Special Award, ANU Productions) and *Wake* (Chamber Made Opera). Film and television credits include: *Don't Go Where I Can't Find You* (Samson Films); *The Passion* (Little Rose Films); *Kathleen was Here* (Treasure Entertainment); *Algorithm* (Copper Alley & Hail Mary Pictures); *Bainne* (Anabasis Films); *Cynthia* (Copper Alley Productions); *Procession* (925 Productions); *The Trap* (Treasure Entertainment); *Away With The Fairies* (Treasure Entertainment); Pebbles (Jonathan Shaw Dir); *Lost in the Living* (Ballyrogan Films); *Children of the Revolution* (RTÉ); and *The Inquiry* (DCTV).

Eimear Farrell has a background in both costume and fashion, which includes design and styling for independent theatre and film productions. Eimear has lent her skills in costume design and wardrobe supervision for numerous theatre, TV and film companies in Dublin and around the world. Over the last decade she has worked alongside the Abbey Theatre and supervised large tours for companies such as Riverdance in Europe, China, America, Japan.

Bryan Burroughs trained in the Samuel Beckett Centre at Trinity College Dublin. Noteworthy performances include *My Foot/My Tutor* (Best Male Performance at Dublin Fringe Festival 2004); Barabbas's *Johnny Patterson : The Singing Irish Clown* (Irish Times Theatre Award Best Supporting Actor 2009) and his self-penned one-man show *Beowulf : The Blockbuster* produced by Pat Moylan which originated as a Show in a Bag and has toured Ireland, Scotland, Wales, France, Australia, New York, was the critics number one success of the Edinburgh Fringe 2014 winning the STAGE Award for Acting Excellence. Other notable productions include Beckett's *Act Without Words 2* for Company SJ which performed at the Barbican in London and the Centre Culturel Irlandais in Paris, Charles Dickens' *A Christmas Carol* with Aaron Monaghan at The Ark and The Pavilion, Quasimodo in *Angela's Ashes : The Musical* in 2017 & 2019, Lenehan in James Joyce's *ULYSSES* at the Abbey Theatre in 2017 & 2018, James Matthews in *14 Voices From The Bloodied Field* directed by Sarah Jane Scaife in 2020. Upcoming productions in 2021 & '22 include TARRY FLYNN with *Livin' Dred, Beowulf : The Blockbuster* and RUNT : *The Boy Who Talked To Dogs* by Amy Conroy with DRAIOCHT/Slingsby Theatre Company. As director, Bryan has directed *Fight Night* and *The Games People Play* for RISE productions written by Gavin Kostick which won Best Actor and the Bewleys Little Gem Award at Dublin Fringe 2010 and Best New Play at the Irish Times Theatre Awards 2013 respectively. Bryan also teaches physical theatre at The Lir Academy of Dramatic Art.

Marie Tierney works both as a designer and production manager for theatre and film. As a production manager, she has toured extensively both nationally and internationally. Credits for Fishamble include *The Alternative*, *Haughey Gregory*, *On Blueberry Hill* and *Rathmines Road*. She has coordinated many large scale and site-specific productions. Previously she has been design coordinator on many productions such as St Patrick's Festival, and a number of site-specific shows in swimming pools with Big Telly, and shows in Kilmainham Gaol, Croke Park and alternative venues around Ireland. She has a particular interest in working in the community and is currently a member of the steering committee for the Creative Places project in Darndale in conjunction with Dublin City Arts Office. As a film designer, she designed costumes for *Borstal Boy*, *Mapmaker*, *Crushproof*, *The Disappearance of Finbar*, *On Home Ground* for RTÉ and many Filmbase shorts. She designed set and costumes for *Kathleen Lynn – The Rebel Doctor* and *James Gandon – A Life* for Loopline Films. She is coordinator on Colaiste Dhulaigh's Performing Arts course and she delivers modules in technical theatre and design. She is a member of the board of directors of Axis Arts in Ballymun and the Association of Irish Stage Technicians, which promotes safety and training in the arts.

Steph Ryan has worked in theatre for many years and with many companies including CoisCéim, Rough Magic, Abbey/Peacock Theatres, OTC and INO to name a few. Work with Fishamble includes: *Handel's Crossing*, *The End of The Road*, *Noah and the Tower Flower*, *Spinning*, *Little Thing Big Thing*, *Invitation to a Journey* (a co-production with CoisCéim, Crash Ensemble and GIAF); *Mainstream*, *Rathmines Road*, *On Blueberry Hill*, *Embargo* and Pat Kinevane's *Forgotten*, *Silent*, *Underneath* and *Before*. She is delighted to be back working with Fishamble on *Duck Duck Goose*.

Sarah Purcell's stage management/ASM credits include: *The Dead* (Breda Cashe Productions 2021); *Transmission* (Dublin Fringe Festival 2020); *To Hell in a Handbag* which originated as a Fishamble Show in a Bag in Dublin Fringe 2016 and has toured both nationally and internationally since. Fishamble: *Embargo* (2020) *Tiny Plays 24/7* (2020); *The Alternative* (2019); *Haughey/Gregory* (2019); *Rathmines Road* (2018). Verdant Productions: *Art* (2021); *Copper Face Jacks: The Musical* (2019); *Signatories* (2016); *The Field* (2015); *Moll* (2014). Cork Opera House: *Aladdin* (2019); *The Wizard of Oz* (2018); *Snow White* (2018); *Cinderella* (2017); *ProdiJIG* (2016). Other: *My Son, My Son* (Project Arts Centre 2018) *The Chastitute* (Gaiety Theatre 2017); *Kings of the Kilburn Highroad* (Livin' Dred 2016); *Freezin'* (Olympia Theatre 2016); *Are You There Garth? It's Me, Margaret* (Pat Egan Productions 2016); *The Bloody Irish!* (Bloody Irish Productions DAC 2015).

Gavin Kostick is Literary Manager at Fishamble, and works with new writers for theatre through a variety of courses, script development workshops and award-winning schemes. Gavin is also an award-winning playwright. His works have been produced nationally and internationally. Favourite works for Fishamble include *The Ash Fire*, *The Flesh Addicts* and *The End of The Road*. Works for other companies include *This is What We Sang* for Kabosh, *Fight Night*, *The Games People Play* and *At the Ford* for RISE Productions and *Gym Swim Party* with Danielle Galligan in co-production with The O'Teilly Theatre. He wrote the libretto for the opera *The Alma Fetish* composed by Raymond Deane, performed at the National Concert Hall. As a performer he performed *Joseph Conrad's Heart of Darkness: Complete*, a six hour show for Absolut Fringe, Dublin Theatre Festival and The London Festival of Literature at the Southbank. He has recently completed a new version of *The Odyssey*, supported by Kilkenny Arts Festival.

DUCK DUCK GOOSE

Caitríona Daly

Characters

CHRIS QUINN, *late twenties, underconfident, vulnerable and kind at times but repressed which often leads to toxic outbursts*

JANE SCULLY, *mid-twenties, her actions could be perceived as dubious but she is also vulnerable with a veneer of toughness*

DAVEY, *late twenties, a good guy who has never had to work too hard to get anything he wanted until now*

ANDY, *late twenties, exudes confidence and never second-guesses himself and is likely to attack if you do it for him*

SARAH, *early thirties, earnest and hardworking but often exasperated at the world and her place within it*

LEO, *late twenties, has spent his life trying to fit in and, as a result, has squeezed himself into any personality anyone wants him to be*

ORLA, *early thirties, always trying her best*

MARIE, *late twenties, spends her life trying to fill the silence, she says stupid things, she always means well*

ALEX, *late thirties, sly and insidious, a demagogue*

KATE, *mid-twenties, a fierce unstoppable young woman*

The actress who plays Jane should also play Orla, Marie and Kate, and the actor who plays Leo also plays Alex.

Setting

Galway, Ireland, 2016–2019

Writer's Note

The play is set in the mind of the character Chris Quinn, as he replays all of his memories that lead him to a certain event. It was the writer's intention that the actor playing Chris changes the set himself at the beginning of every new scene as he is physically trying to reconstruct what has occurred. The actors (with the exception of Chris) and props should have different roles and uses throughout the different scenes to play on the idea of headspace and the tangible and often deceptive nature of memories.

" " Quotation marks are used to indicate when something from the past is being repeated.

This text went to press before the end of rehearsals and so may differ slightly from the play as performed.

Scene One

*The aftermath of a party in a sparse living room, May 2016.
CHRIS QUINN is asleep on an armchair. It is 6.10 a.m. He
awakes. He has a penis drawn on his face. JANE SCULLY
stands at the door. He looks around, she gives him a fright.*

JANE. Sorry.

CHRIS. No, I'm sorry, you just gave me a fright that's all.

JANE. I didn't mean to.

CHRIS. Of course not.

An awkward silence.

What time is it there?

JANE. Ten past six.

CHRIS. Jesus.

Pause.

JANE. Do you mind if I get something to drink?

CHRIS. Not my flat, you don't need my permission.

JANE. Right, yeah.

JANE goes to the fridge.

CHRIS. Wouldn't expect much in there other than a couple of
cans really. Davey and Andy have shares in Domino's at this
point.

JANE. Domino's?

CHRIS. Pizza.

JANE. Oh, yeah.

CHRIS. Have I been asleep for long or?

JANE. Long enough to have a penis drawn on your face.

CHRIS. Oh for fuck... not again.

CHRIS stands and goes to the mirror.

JANE. I think it suits you.

CHRIS looks at JANE.

I'm joking.

CHRIS. Sorry.

Beat.

I was just being a dickhead.

They laugh.

Awkward.

I'll have some water if you're having one.

JANE. Sure.

JANE opens a press looking for glasses.

A mug, a bowl and a bottle of Toilet Duck.

CHRIS. I'll leave the Toilet Duck to you, I had a couple of pints of bleach earlier, so, don't want to be greedy.

JANE. You had a quacking good time then?

CHRIS. Mad for the quack.

JANE. Bowl it is so.

JANE pours water into the mug and bowl and hands the bowl to CHRIS. They drink.

CHRIS. Did you have a good night?

JANE. Eh...

CHRIS. I know what you mean.

JANE. Yeah.

CHRIS. All nights out feel the same once you turn twenty-five.

JANE. Maybe.

CHRIS. I'm sorry but what's your name again? I know I've met you before, I just, I've an awful memory.

JANE. It's Jane, Chris.

CHRIS. Jane? Sorry, we could've been in school together for all I know, and I still would've forgotten.

JANE. We were in school together, I was your teacher.

Beat.

CHRIS. What?

JANE. I'm messing with you.

CHRIS. Did I mention I was gullible too?

JANE. We have met though, a few times.

CHRIS. I thought as much.

JANE. You're always kind of quiet, to be fair.

CHRIS. That's me I suppose.

JANE. Not that you'd get a word in edgeways with that lot.

CHRIS. A crazy crew alright.

JANE. Were you there the night of Fiona's house-warming? It was months ago now.

CHRIS. I don't think so.

JANE. Are you sure? The Guards arrived after karaoke broke out into a fist fight? That's why they call Squee 'Garth Hooks' now.

JANE *air-boxes*.

CHRIS....

JANE (*singing*). I got friends in low places... That's what he was singing, when the fight started.

CHRIS. I wasn't there when it happened.

JANE. Oh.

CHRIS. But I definitely remember hearing about it.

JANE. Really?

CHRIS. I might've been there earlier that night?

JANE. I thought I saw you.

CHRIS. I try my best not to be conspicuous.

JANE. Whereas I... don't.

Beat.

Rocked up to work the next day stinking.

CHRIS. Not too happy with you?

JANE. Are they ever? PWC aren't the worst, though.

CHRIS. You're an accountant then?

JANE. Oh no, mainly admin stuff, secretarial, but they don't call it that any more.

CHRIS. Right.

Awkward pause.

JANE. Of course I'm sure you saw pictures of me that night, the karaoke one. Even if you didn't see me in the flesh.

CHRIS. No... what?

JANE. The photo that Davey took, of me.

CHRIS....

JANE. It was hardly a nude now but.

CHRIS. I don't know what you're talking about.

JANE. Sure you do. The one where I was sitting on the couch and my nipple had popped out.

CHRIS....No.

JANE. I think he captioned it: I'd fuck the shit out of Jane Scully's tits.

CHRIS. I swear, I don't know what you're talking about.

JANE. Sure you do; it was in your little WhatsApp group.

CHRIS. No. It wasn't.

JANE. Do you think we don't know? About your WhatsApp group? That we're stupid? All your little pictures. They get screenshotted you know.

CHRIS. I'm in a WhatsApp group but all we really talk about is like FIFA and chicken wings. We might talk about girls the odd time but no pictures, not like that, I swear.

JANE. Well if you won't even admit it exists.

CHRIS. I swear, I swear to you. I have never seen a photo of you or any of the girls in that group honestly.

JANE. Well there must be another group then.

CHRIS. I don't think so.

JANE. Whatever.

CHRIS. I'm sorry that happened.

JANE. What are you sorry for, Chris? You didn't do it.

CHRIS. No but.

JANE. But your friend Davey did.

CHRIS. He definitely didn't. I think I'd remember a text like that.

JANE. Well don't defend him.

CHRIS. But I don't know what you're talking about?

Beat.

JANE. Sorry. I shouldn't've made it awkward; it was months ago now anyway and I'm hardly one to be talking.

CHRIS. It's okay.

JANE. I mean, I'm still here amn't I? Still going to ye're parties. Still… you know.

Awkward pause.

CHRIS. Sleeping with him?

JANE. What do you mean by that?

CHRIS. I mean you got off with him last night, right?

JANE. 'Got off'?

CHRIS. I was just asking.

JANE. 'Just asking'?

CHRIS. Look, I'm sorry. I just know you were kissing him so considering you're still here, I assumed.

JANE. Assumed what?

CHRIS non-verbally insinuates sex, JANE bats it off dismissively.

So sleeping with him would excuse the photo he took of me?

CHRIS. I'm not saying that.

JANE. Well you were saying something.

CHRIS. All I know is I've never seen that photo.

Awkward pause.

JANE. I better go.

JANE stands still.

CHRIS. See you then.

JANE. Do you know him well?

CHRIS. Davey? He's my best friend.

JANE. And has he had many girlfriends or?

CHRIS. A few, he's hardly a player now.

JANE. And the other one?

CHRIS. Andy? He has a girlfriend, yeah.

JANE. How well do you know him?

CHRIS. Well enough, more Davey's mate to be honest.

JANE. Can I have his phone number?

CHRIS. Andy?

JANE. No, Davey.

CHRIS. I eh… I don't think so.

JANE. Why not?

CHRIS. It's not really mine to give.

JANE. What do you think I'm going to do with it?

CHRIS. Nothing, it's just not mine to hand out that's all.

Beat.

JANE. Well can I have yours then?

CHRIS *looks to* JANE, *uneasy.*

We're friends now, aren't we?

CHRIS. Yeah.

JANE. So can I have it?

CHRIS. Is everything okay?

JANE. Everything's fine, can I have your phone number?

CHRIS. Sure, it's 0874365789.

JANE *dials the number on her phone.*

JANE. It's not ringing.

JANE *points to* CHRIS*'s phone on the table.*

CHRIS. Oh sorry, what number did I give you?

JANE. 0874365789.

CHRIS. Sorry, it's 788, I always do this, it's muscle-memory, psychosomatic or something, 7-8-9.

JANE. Psychosomatic… Sure.

CHRIS. Genuinely a mistake.

JANE. Whatever.

An awkward pause.

I'm going.

CHRIS. Goodbye.

JANE stands still.

JANE. You should know, Chris.

A change.

Pricks like that, always get what's coming to them.

It begins.

Scene Two

DAVEY *and* ANDY*'s living room, later that day.* DAVEY *and* ANDY *are sitting down.* CHRIS *stands near the door. It is tense. Every nervous tic any of them have is in overdrive.*

DAVEY. And you saw her?

CHRIS. Yes, I told you that. You saw it in the WhatsApp for Christ's sake.

DAVEY. But that's what I mean. You saw her, so you know.

CHRIS. Know what?

ANDY. That she's a fucking crackpot.

DAVEY. Andy.

ANDY. Do you think somebody sane would do this?

CHRIS. I don't see how me seeing her before she left has anything to do with the WhatsApp messages?

DAVEY. What I mean is you know she was fine, you saw her. You know she was making it up.

Pause.

CHRIS. Well, is she?

DAVEY. How can you ask me that?

CHRIS. I don't know, I just… Did you do something that maybe she took up the wrong way?

DAVEY. I didn't even have sex with her, Chris.

ANDY. And I didn't expose myself to her either.

DAVEY. Well…

ANDY. What?

DAVEY. You kind of did.

ANDY. I went into you, looking for a condom. If she walked in on me in the bathroom, would I be exposing myself to her then too?

CHRIS. Condom? I didn't think Ais was out last night.

ANDY. She wasn't.

CHRIS. So…

ANDY. Who I have in my bedroom is my business.

CHRIS. But she did see you with your…

DAVEY. Well I certainly did.

ANDY. And who's to say what I saw then, heh?

DAVEY. Andy.

ANDY. You better remember that I'm the only one saw you in that room. For all I know you were in there doing all sorts to her.

DAVEY. Fuck off, Andy. You know I didn't, I didn't, rape, her.

ANDY. Well if she's not lying about me then how can I be so sure?

DAVEY. The point is that you saw her, Chris. You spoke to her, didn't you?

CHRIS. Yes.

DAVEY. And she was fine?

CHRIS. I suppose.

DAVEY. You suppose?

CHRIS. It was six o'clock in the morning, Davey.

DAVEY. But she wasn't crying or hurt or?

CHRIS. No.

DAVEY. Good, that's good.

CHRIS. Is it?

DAVEY. I mean, it's good that you know that she was fine, okay? That's what I mean.

CHRIS. Yeah.

DAVEY. That you know I didn't do that to her, that I couldn't.

CHRIS. Yeah.

DAVEY looks at CHRIS.

I know you wouldn't do that.

DAVEY. Thank you, Chris. I'm sorry you've been dragged into this.

CHRIS. My good luck I suppose.

ANDY. Surprised she hasn't said you assaulted her too.

CHRIS. Well why would she say that? I was only talking to her.

ANDY. Why would she say any of it? 'Cause she's a nutter I suppose.

CHRIS. Maybe.

There is a tense silence. ANDY glares at DAVEY.

DAVEY. Chris?

CHRIS. What?

DAVEY. I need you to delete the WhatsApp group.

CHRIS. Why?

ANDY. You know why.

DAVEY. Andy.

CHRIS. I don't see why you need me to do that?

DAVEY. Because it won't look good.

CHRIS. Won't look good to who?

DAVEY. If she's gone to the Guards like she says she has, it won't look good.

CHRIS. They're not going to go after your phone, Davey. You haven't done anything. They won't look that far into it.

DAVEY. But what if they do?

CHRIS. Well just delete the messages then.

ANDY. You can only delete them for seven minutes after you sent them. You're the group admin, so.

CHRIS. They're not going to pontificate over what you meant when you said an 'O'Carroll Special'.

ANDY. Sounds like sex to me.

CHRIS. Yeah well it sounds like a Supermac's order *to me*.

ANDY (*to* DAVEY). And what about Player 3? You're not the only one implicated in those messages.

DAVEY (*to* CHRIS). You don't exactly come off great in them either.

CHRIS. What's that supposed to mean?

DAVEY. I'm just saying, you're no model citizen.

CHRIS. I still haven't been accused of raping someone though, have I?

DAVEY. Will you stop… I did not… Stop saying that.

CHRIS. I'm not the one saying it. She is.

DAVEY. I am aware of what she's saying.

CHRIS. I'm sorry, Davey. I just don't see why you need me to get involved.

DAVEY. I don't need you to get involved. I need you to delete the WhatsApp group. That's all.

CHRIS. Even if I did delete the group, they'd still find them. There's clouds now. Nothing's ever really deleted.

DAVEY. They're not going to get as far as clouds because I didn't do anything but if the messages are there…

CHRIS. They might wonder.

DAVEY. Exactly.

Beat.

Look, I'm sorry for stressing you. I'm just… I don't know what's happening and I'm freaking out and I don't know what to do.

CHRIS. I know, it's just the past fourteen hours are a bit of a blur and…

DAVEY. I know and I know I'm asking a lot.

CHRIS. Yeah.

ANDY. It's not a lot.

DAVEY. Andy.

ANDY. It's not, it's not a lot to ask. I deleted Sex-Men, I don't see why he has a problem deleting Boyzone or whatever the fuck the group's called.

DAVEY. Will you just shut up.

CHRIS. Sex-Men?

ANDY. Sex-Men, like X-Men.

CHRIS. Yeah I got that, Andy, but what the fuck is it?

ANDY. It's a WhatsApp group, Chris. And I deleted it.

CHRIS. What?

CHRIS *looks at his phone.*

ANDY. I'm sorry are you looking for a fucking invitation?

CHRIS. No… I just never heard about it before.

DAVEY. You wouldn't like it, Chris. It's stupid. I don't even like it.

CHRIS. What is it then?

ANDY. Anecdotes, a few jokes, some edgier content. We talk about birds, Chris. Women. We're not sure you've ever met one so we didn't want to scare you.

DAVEY. Didn't think you'd be into it.

CHRIS. Who else is in the group?

ANDY. Me, Davey, Hugh, Squee, Mark, Damien and Twixy.

DAVEY. You're just not an arsehole so I didn't think…

CHRIS. Probably the first time someone's been excluded for not being an arsehole so thank you, David. God knows by the looks of things I'm already in one too many WhatsApp groups.

DAVEY. Chris.

CHRIS. All beginning to make a bit more sense though.

ANDY. What makes sense?

CHRIS (*to* DAVEY). She brought it up last night, your group. I didn't know anything about it. Said you took a picture of her with her tit out last year in a karaoke bar. Something about 'fucking her tits'. I said I'd never seen it. Not in our WhatsApp group.

DAVEY. When have I ever been in a karaoke bar?

ANDY *and* DAVEY *exchange a very subtle look.*

CHRIS. Are you sure you didn't?

DAVEY. What do you take me for?

CHRIS. Well someone took a photo of her and she wasn't happy about it.

ANDY. Maybe that's what all this is about then.

CHRIS *and* DAVEY *look to* ANDY.

Revenge.

CHRIS. A bit far for revenge, Andy.

ANDY. Maybe not to a nutter like her.

DAVEY. I don't know why she'd be taking revenge on me, I didn't do it.

CHRIS. Well she thinks you did.

ANDY. You would, to be fair. Fuck her tits. She should take it as a compliment.

DAVEY. Well I wouldn't.

ANDY. I meant it rhetorically.

DAVEY. Well don't.

ANDY. Because girls are so innocent? My dick's been shown to half the female population of Galway at this stage.

CHRIS. Ais must be very proud.

ANDY. I don't give two hoots about it. She can show who she likes.

CHRIS. At least *they* have your permission.

ANDY. And what's that supposed to mean?

CHRIS. It means you sent it.

ANDY. Alright, Jesus. Do you need a hand getting off that cross?

DAVEY. Will the two of you just leave it?

Beat.

Look, Chris. I don't care whether you delete the group or not. I just need to hear you say you believe me. You've known me my whole life. Would you be friends with someone capable of doing that? What she said...

CHRIS. No.

DAVEY. See.

CHRIS. I believe you.

DAVEY. Thank you. And I didn't mean to put you under pressure, about deleting the group. I was just panicked. I'm sure you're right, it'll blow over. I didn't do anything, after all.

CHRIS. Thanks, yeah, I just, it's been a day and I'm not sure... I just need to sleep and –

DAVEY. I know.

ANDY. No.

DAVEY. What?

ANDY. No, he does it now or else.

CHRIS. Or else what?

ANDY. Or else you're both under a bus.

CHRIS *and* DAVEY *look at each other.*

DAVEY. Andy?

ANDY. Well if 'help me best friend', 'I love you best friend' isn't going to work then something better.

DAVEY. That wasn't what I was doing.

ANDY. Well it certainly sounded like it.

DAVEY. I think if today has established anything, it's that a lot of things sound like things they don't.

ANDY. Easy for you to say. I'm the one whose role is explicitly stated in those text messages. 'Player 3'? Whereas you, 'The O'Carroll Special'? You're a fucking joke.

DAVEY. Fuck off, Andy.

ANDY (*to* DAVEY). No. He deletes the group or else. For all I know you were in that room doing all sorts to her, I only came in to see if she was okay.

CHRIS. Andy…

ANDY. I might send a few texts out of my own. Who's to say I haven't already. God knows it's taking him long enough to make up his mind, you wouldn't know what I was doing.

DAVEY. You wouldn't do that.

ANDY. If that's a chance you're willing to take.

DAVEY. You're a sad prick, Andrew. Do you know that?

ANDY. A sad prick who's got your bollocks in an organ grinder though.

DAVEY is out of steam. ANDY *looks to* CHRIS *and* DAVEY.

CHRIS. I don't know what you're getting so worked up over, Andy. I was gonna do it anyway.

DAVEY. Chris…

CHRIS. I was going to do it anyway.

Lights dim.

DAVEY *and* ANDY *exit.* CHRIS *begins to rearrange the set.*

Text messages are projected in front of CHRIS, *he stands and looks at them. They are heard through a voice-over.*

Boyz In Da Snood

Chris
Jesus what did you do to that fucking nutjob?

Davey
The old O'Carroll Special what?

Squee
Ladies love cool O'Carroll…

Davey
What the fuck have I gotten myself into now? [laughing face emoji]

Chris
You're a bigger nutjob for going down there with that [aubergine emoji] in the first place. I met her on her way out your front door, a complete wreck the head.

Simon
No one knows head like Jane Scully.

Davey
Well she didn't wreck the head last night at least! [tongue emoji]

Squee
Sounds like a satisfied customer, she was lit enough so was she?

Davey
Was she fuck, a fire extinguisher more like.

Chris
A worthy opponent for your fire hose anyway

Davey
I do what I can when I can get it.

Andy
And she definitely got it.

Davey
Oh she got it, we were having so much fun at one point, Andy thought he might join in. Isn't that right Player 3?

Squee
Aisling will have your balls in a harness, Andy.

Andy
Like anyone would believe a word coming out of that bint's mouth.

Chris
Yeah, it's a pity you didn't fuck the crazy out of her, O'Carroll.

Davey
It'd take a gang bang to do that, do you want in, Quinn?

Andy
Quinn wouldn't know what to make of a gang bang.
Probably end up screwing the keyhole. [aubergine emoji]
[door emoji]

Chris
This Quinn is so not in.

Twixy
All out of O'Carroll's Meats so? [laughing face emoji]

Davey
Sold out.

Chris
I'd say it is, poor girl could hardly walk.

Davey
The O'Carroll Special never fails.

Squee
Do you want fries with that?[fries emoji]

Conor
O'Carroll's Meats [crazy laughing face emoji]

Chris
Good man Mark.

Davey
Good girl Jane.

Chris
I hope you perverts are cleaning up that crime scene anyway.
I'll give you a shout later. Also cheers for the Michelangelo
that was left on my face. [aubergine emoji]

Switch screen to the texts sent from JANE.

_0851234567_
Hi, it's Jane, from last night. Your friend Davey raped me
and his friend Andy tried as much. I'm going to the Guards.
I wanted to tell him myself but you wouldn't give me his
number.

...

...

Three dots appear on screen implying CHRIS _is replying but_
then they disappear. CHRIS _returns to Boyz In Da Snood,_
deletes all of the messages and then deletes the group.

CHRIS _rearranges the set and, using a can of spray-paint,_
he sprays the word 'RAPIST!' on the back wall of the set.

Scene Three

Two months later. The ramshackle office of Quinn Paints LTD.
CHRIS *sits at his desk,* SARAH *stands glaring at him and*
pointing at the spray-paint on the wall. It is tense.

SARAH. Why did you delete the WhatsApp group?

CHRIS. Eh I don't think that's the point right now, Sarah.

SARAH. I mean Jesus would you look at the place for God's
sake, do you not see what you've done?

CHRIS. What I've done? Are you mad? I've done nothing.

SARAH. You know what I mean!

CHRIS. What, I broke into my own office and spray-painted the
word 'rapist' on the wall?

SARAH. I'm not sure right now is the best time to be a smart-
arse, Chris. Dad's having a caliption inside.

CHRIS. Conniption.

SARAH. What?

CHRIS. He's having a conniption not a caliption.

SARAH. I don't think that's the word you need to be most
concerned about right now.

Beat.

CHRIS. Did they take much stock?

SARAH. I don't think stealing cans of paint was on their
agenda, no.

CHRIS. Intersectional feminists, Sarah, you wouldn't know
what they're capable of.

SARAH. Yeah, well, they've infiltrated the company whoever
they are, the CCTV footage has mysteriously disappeared.

CHRIS. An opportunity for Dad to do his Poirot impression at
least.

SARAH. This isn't funny, Chris.

CHRIS. I know, *Sarah*, there's no need to be so patronising.

SARAH. The picket outside they had was bad but this is, this is next-level.

CHRIS. This is slander.

SARAH. Slander?

CHRIS. I'm not a rapist.

SARAH. No, Chris, you're not Hitler but you're fucking Goebbels aren't you?

CHRIS. I'm Goebbels? That girl's gone all round Galway telling anyone who'll listen that Davey's raped her but I'm Goebbels?

Pause.

You do know Davey did not do that? You do know that she's lying?

SARAH. That's not the point.

CHRIS. Not the point? Of course it's the point. You're going around acting like I'm some sort of criminal. I haven't done anything.

SARAH. You disposed of evidence for a rape case, Chris, I think that's something!

CHRIS. It's not a rape case. She's gone to the Guards and they're investigating, the DPP will never pick it up. They only take up things in the public eye. Never mind a false accusation.

SARAH. And what makes you so confident it's false?

Pause.

CHRIS. Because I was there, I saw her.

SARAH. You saw 'that fucking nutjob'?

CHRIS. Yes, I did, actually. And she might've been strange but she was not hurt and she was not traumatised.

SARAH. How do you know?

CHRIS. Again, because I was there.

SARAH. Well those text messages suggest something else.

CHRIS. The text messages don't suggest anything of the sort.

SARAH. No, just that you're scumbags, really. And now the whole of Galway knows about it. I got sent them screenshots by about five different people before anyone copped it was my brother.

CHRIS. Fiona saw them on Squee's phone, she thought Andy had cheated on Ais and that Ais might want to know about it so she screenshotted them.

SARAH. I don't care why they were sent. I care that my friends now think that my brother is an arsehole.

CHRIS. I am not an arsehole.

SARAH. Then why did you say those things?

CHRIS *has no response. He tries to shake it off.*

CHRIS. You don't get it.

SARAH. So explain it to me.

CHRIS. She's out for revenge.

SARAH. Really, is she?

CHRIS. Someone took a photo of her, her tit was out, she thinks Davey took it.

SARAH. And this is how she's getting revenge? She could just key his car, Chris.

CHRIS. Well Davey didn't rape her, so?

SARAH *doesn't respond.*

You think he did it. You think he's a liar.

SARAH. I haven't said that.

CHRIS. Why else would you be going on like this, you've made up your mind.

SARAH. I haven't. I'm just struggling with it.

CHRIS. Do you think I would've gone to all this trouble, if I wasn't sure of what had happened? I was there for fuck's sake.

SARAH *thinks about this for a second.*

Well don't bother defending me.

SARAH. It's not that. You're a good person. I know that. I just sometimes...

CHRIS. You sometimes what?

SARAH. I sometimes worry, that you're a bit led that's all.

CHRIS. 'Led'?

SARAH. I don't recognise that person in those messages, Chris. I don't recognise him.

CHRIS. So?

SARAH. So why would you talk like that if you weren't being a bit led?

CHRIS. Oh that's such a fucking cop-out. I talk how I want when I want. I am not a child. I do not need to be patronised like this by my own sister.

SARAH. Okay, fine. I'm sorry. I'm worried. That's all.

CHRIS. Don't be.

SARAH. How can I not be? This isn't just about you any more. Between the pickets and the break-in, the business, we're in trouble. It's not as easy as me saying I believe you, Chris. Which I do by the way. I'm struggling but I trust you. But there's a bigger picture now too. It mightn't've been your ideal scenario to end up in the family business but it's Dad's and it's mine too. I don't have a swanky CV to rely on, impressive references and a degree in commerce. You'll be fine if it goes under but I won't and it's Dad's life's work. All gone. Just like that.

Pause.

CHRIS. I know and I'm sorry. I didn't think for a second it would lead to this.

SARAH. How could you?

CHRIS. I never wanted this to affect any of you.

SARAH. I know that.

Beat.

And me and Dad and Mam even, we've been talking.

CHRIS. About what?

SARAH. Just hear me out.

CHRIS....

SARAH. You could apologise. Make a statement. Saying you're sorry you deleted the messages. You haven't really done anything, Chris. You're not the one. Your accusation, it's not the same. People would –

CHRIS. No.

SARAH. Please.

CHRIS. I haven't done anything wrong and Davey hasn't done anything wrong. I'm not admitting guilt when I haven't done anything.

SARAH. I know, I understand and I'm not asking for an admission, no one's saying that but a few words to say you're sorry for upset caused or something?

CHRIS. I'm not sorry, Sarah.

SARAH. Chris –

CHRIS. And the only apologising that should be going on around here is whichever idiot broke into someone's office and defamed him with a crime he's never even been accused of!

Beat.

SARAH. I was just asking.

CHRIS. 'Just asking'?

Beat.

SARAH. We have to do something.

CHRIS. Well I won't be doing anything of the sort.

SARAH *leaves*. CHRIS *rearranges the set*.

Scene Four

Four months later. A local radio station. It is late. CHRIS *is sat on a chair waiting.* LEO *arrives, he is the presenter, larger-than-life and what he lacks in charm he makes up for in enthusiasm.*

LEO. Christopher Christopherson! My man! How's it going!

CHRIS. Hi Leo.

LEO. Good to have you in the casa, hombre.

CHRIS. Well, thanks for… thanks for doing this, for having me on. No one else seemed to be giving me a look-in, so…

LEO. What a year for you, my man, what a year for you. Sure I can't quite get over it myself, poor Davo and Ando, the boys, man. They wouldn't be up to much like, wouldn't need to be doing that now would they? Not you anyway, Chris, we know you're not like that any route.

CHRIS. Eh… no. Probably not.

LEO. Happy to give you this dig-out with the ol' PR shizz though. Collo says you've been feeling the burn, the old radical women's groups got you down I hear.

CHRIS. They're picketing… outside… Dad's… the business, struggling a bit I suppose. I wasn't inclined to do much now till last week. I had thought it might die down but they put a rock through a car driving into our premises, hit one of our employees and she's in hospital now so… here I am.

LEO. Happy to help. Who'da thought in school ten years ago that the lads would be up for rape, you'd be helping them and that I'd have my own show on Galway's third-most-listened-to radio station. Mad! Not sure they'd be calling me 'Sergeant Nonce' too quickly if they'd known.

CHRIS. Yeah, it's, mad, I suppose.

LEO. Sergeant Nonce takes centre-stage.

Beat.

Sergeant Nonce… ha? Where did you ever come up with that like?

CHRIS. I didn't come up with it…

LEO. Thought it might've been a compliment for a while, army man, macho. Until my dad kindly filled me in on it being another word for a paedo! Ha! Nonce! What was I like, going around thinking you'd be doing me a solid with a name like that!

CHRIS. I didn't come up with it so…

LEO. Still chanted it though didn't you? Beside your pals, SERGEANT NONCE! You did though, I remember, didn't you?

CHRIS. I don't think I did… I know they called you that but I don't think I –

LEO. Hombre, it's been a whole ten years don't worry about it. Not going to carry that one around now am I, ha? Amn't I not? Not when I'm living the life. Chilling here with the career trajectory of an out-and-out radio star, ha? No video is going to be killing this dude am I right?

Beat.

CHRIS. It's going well then?

LEO. Oh I've a foot in the door, it's more about shimmying the rest of me in at this point and I mean radio's cool, man. And Ireland's still mad for it isn't she? Yeah it'll do for now but what I'm thinking next is TRUE-CRIME PODCASTS.

LEO *gestures to* CHRIS *to be impressed.*

Yeah you've seen them, you know the ones.

CHRIS. Yeah.

LEO. Murders… disappearances… bank robberies, CORRUPT GOVERNMENTS and then the presenter – BANG – solves it themselves. Ha? Now that, that's what you're after.

CHRIS. Great.

Beat.

LEO. Anyway, I've got the legal deets down, my man, alright? You're not to be influencing any juries with any evidence.

Not allowed, comprende, bro? No contempt of court to be
going on here. Don't want to be doing anything that might
get you wrapped up in an old En-ye song em-kay?

CHRIS. What?

LEO (*to the tune of Enya's song 'Orinoco Flow'*). Jail away, jail
away, jail away…

CHRIS. Cool.

LEO. But seriously, this is not about your crime. We're not
discussing your charges we just want to hear about your
damn-near-crumbling family business. We'll be leaving the
trial and those naughty texts alone but to be fair, total nutjob
of a chick I'd say, was she? Boiling your *balls* more like,
fuck boiling the *bunny*.

CHRIS. Well no not really.

LEO. You said that in the texts man though? Nutjob.

CHRIS. She was a bit odd.

LEO. A total fucking nutjob you said.

CHRIS. She wasn't a nutjob.

CHRIS *has become very conscious of the technicians listening
and is physically trying to block their conversation off.*

Can you lower your voice… Please?

LEO. No one's recording you, we're not on-air… yet! And
anyway they're your words, dude, not mine. We've all seen
them, the texts, sure they've been screenshotted to every
WhatsApp group this side of the Shannon what? I know a
few lads, recite them off in nightclubs, man, for the craic
like, party piece. Before the Guards started taking her
seriously though, after that it just felt criminal.

CHRIS (*sarcastically*). Oh well that's great, you must thank
them for me.

LEO. Ah no, I didn't mean to be getting you all riled up. We're
here for your family, we're here to save the institution that is
QUINN PAINTS LIMITED.

CHRIS. Thanks.

LEO. Great, great. You know, I get it and I love it. Think we're coming up to broadcast anyway so you ready to go? Get those flaps onto you!

CHRIS *looks at him, puzzled.* LEO *points to the headphones.*

Muffs, my man, muffs. Back in three Proseccos!

LEO *exits briefly and comes back to the seat opposite* CHRIS. *He puts on headphones and does vocal exercises into the mics.* LEO *sounds like a completely different person on air. Garth Brooks' song 'Friends in Low Places' plays out.*

VOICE-OVER. And we're good in five, four, three, two –

LEO. Hello and welcome to this week's edition of *News Boost.* On tonight's show we discuss Brexit Trouble: Is it May Day all over again for Theresa and just how many times can media outlets get away with using this pun? And coming up in part two, Rogue Farmers in Roscommon: We ask why would anyone go to this much trouble to make an X-men out of hay bales? But first on tonight's show we have Chris Quinn. Chris has been buzzing around as your friendly neighbourhood cyberman for the past few months, as screenshots from a WhatsApp group he was a member of went viral due to a rape allegation that had been brought against his friend. Resulting in a split of opinions in the city of tribes and making what could have been a relatively private case a SALACIOUS page-turner or should I say scroller. Am I right, Chris Quinn? Thanks for coming on the show.

CHRIS *is scowling at* LEO.

CHRIS. Thanks for having me on, Leo.

LEO. Now, I won't lie to you, Chris. It was a bit of a shock, you wanting to come talk to me on – (*In a radio-announcer voice.*) Le-le-le-like a G6fm Galway's Premier Rockathon. Were you following legal advice?

CHRIS. I'm not here about the trial, Leo. I've explained that to you previously.

LEO. So you weren't or you were?

CHRIS. Again, this isn't about that. Legal advice doesn't come into it. This is about –

LEO. Very daring move, my man.

CHRIS. I don't, I'm not / here about that.

LEO. Running to the boys' defence. Propping your boys up, Chris.

CHRIS *looks at* LEO *alarmingly.*

CHRIS. I'm here to talk about my family business which has been picketed every day for six straight months now.

LEO. Now, from what I've gathered from your texts there were a few of you in the room when the alleged happened, is that something you do often, you and your boys? Watch, is it? Getting off on the birds or each other?

CHRIS. They're not my boys and I don't want to talk about / that, I've told you.

LEO. Ah, they're your special somethings though aren't they, Chris?

CHRIS. Somebody last week threw a large / rock.

LEO. So you weren't in the room?

CHRIS. They threw a large rock at an employee's car when she / was driving in.

LEO. And what has you so sure that she wasn't raped? What made you jump to their defence? A bit strange having previously described the aftermath as a 'crime scene', what changed?

CHRIS. Our employee, she was driving in to work and now she's in hospital, she's injured and / this has to stop.

LEO. The girl in question is in hospital?

CHRIS. Yes.

LEO. The girl your friends assaulted is in hospital and you're still defending them?

CHRIS. No that's not what I'm saying, our employee, one of our employees is now in hospital from the rock, the crash, from the protesters, and / it's not fair.

LEO. And your friend Davey?

CHRIS. She's been seriously injured and we're asking for this to / end now.

LEO. Did Davey end up in hospital too?

CHRIS. No... what?

LEO. In the messages he seems to insinuate that he had fornicated with a fire extinguisher so I mean, I'm not quite sure how that works but it's got to hurt. Is that something he'd done before? Penetrated an inanimate object?

A switch has flipped in CHRIS. *He is visibly reaching boiling point but trying to remain calm.*

CHRIS (*concentrated*). I want people to leave my family alone, they haven't done anything wrong and I haven't done anything wrong and / I told you I didn't want –

LEO. I imagine a hoover might be more practical in the long run has he tried a hoover? Penetrating a hoover? Perhaps, you yourself might be able to recommend a preferred – (*Reading from his notes.*) door handle?

CHRIS. You're taking this all out of context that's not... This... I'm not apologising but this is on me, not my family and I think it's grossly unfair that you've / brought me on here –

LEO. And what about the tears?

CHRIS. What tears?

LEO. The tears in her vaginal wall? Sorry for the graphics, folks!

CHRIS. What?

LEO. I had the opportunity to obtain her patient's report from the sexual assault unit in Galway University Hospital today, have you seen it yourself?

CHRIS. No?

CHRIS looks lost and frightened.

LEO. Did she hide that well, Chris, her ripped vagina? Or did you delete that too?

CHRIS. That's not true, I was there, she was fine, I saw her, it's not true, there were no tears.

LEO. The nutjob just did it to herself is that it?

CHRIS. I didn't actually mean she was a nutjob / it was a turn of phrase.

LEO. But you text it, Chris. You text it and then you deleted all of the texts and the WhatsApp group. But there was another WhatsApp group, wasn't there?

CHRIS....Yes.

LEO. But you didn't delete that one.

CHRIS. No.

LEO. And why was that?

CHRIS. Because I... I wasn't in it.

LEO. Okay, okay, they left you out of that one did they? Your boys. Well that's a relief. Isn't it?

CHRIS *doesn't respond. Dead air. The technician indicates to* LEO *to move it along.*

Well look, let me lay this to you plain, Chris. You didn't rape the girl. I'm not angry at you, nobody's angry at you, okay? I think you're a bit of an idiot for deleting that WhatsApp group and I struggle to see your need to stand up for these douchebags but nobody is angry at you, we all just want you to catch yourself on a bit.

CHRIS. I'm an idiot?

LEO. It was an idiotic thing to do.

CHRIS. I'm not the one going round screaming 'braw!' and 'man' and 'dude' at everyone I see in the hopes of disguising the fact that I haven't got a personality.

LEO. Alright, man, chill out...

CHRIS. But I'm an idiot?

CHRIS *begins to take* LEO*'s headphones and microphone off him as he screams the next part into* LEO*'s face.* JANE *singing 'Friends in Low Places' plays distortedly.*

Some venomous man-hating slut is defaming my best friends but I'm an awful person for having their back? They can get fucked whenever they want, do you think they need to do that? They don't need to force anyone. There were no rips, no tears that night, no pain, for all we know she went at herself with a fucking hacksaw.

A white-noise ringing sound floods the stage, giving the impression that they may have been pulled off the air or that CHRIS *has come to. The tension clears up.*

LEO *sits back in the chair smugly and shrugs his shoulders.*

LEO. Whoaaaaaaaaaaa. This one's gonna be huge, man, it's going down in the motherfucking books. Legendary. You were a total 'nutjob' yourself, what?

LEO *gets up out of his chair and heads for the door.*

And look, I am sorry for what's going on, with you and that stuff. I'm sorry for that interview even, well maybe I'm not sorry for that but you need to understand… we can't be seen to be supporting those guys, not in this climate. And I forgive you for saying I don't have a personality but I really meant no harm… well, maybe, a little but what else can you expect from Sergeant Nonce, ha?

Pause. A brief moment of sincerity.

You're not a bad guy, Chris, you never were but even you have to realise eventually, nine times out of ten, if it talks like a duck, it's a duck.

LEO *goes to exit, pauses.*

Quack.

CHRIS*, in a violent rage, starts moving the set around him.*

Scene Five

Two months later. CHRIS *and* DAVEY *sit at a high table in their local pub/club.* DAVEY, *paranoid, is keeping a watchful eye on everything around them.* CHRIS, *pretends to watch a football match on a large screen.* DAVEY *goes to say something.*

CHRIS. This is fine.

DAVEY....

CHRIS. It's fine.

DAVEY. People are looking.

CHRIS. Let them.

DAVEY. I didn't want to do this, Chris.

CHRIS. No point in hiding.

DAVEY. I'm not hiding. I just don't want to be here.

CHRIS (*shouting at the TV*). Are you blind, ref?

DAVEY. I'm going to head off.

CHRIS. You're not.

DAVEY. You can't make me stay here.

CHRIS, *who hasn't taken his eyes off the TV since the beginning of the scene, turns and looks* DAVEY *directly in the eye.*

CHRIS. I think you owe me more than a few favours at this stage, actually.

CHRIS *goes back to the TV screen.* DAVEY *retreats, begrudgingly.*

DAVEY. I didn't make you do anything, Chris. And I certainly didn't ask you to make a tit out of yourself on the radio.

CHRIS. He was a snake. I told you that. I'm not talking about this any more.

DAVEY. Why did you do it? Leo was a snide arsehole in school, he was hardly going to be much better on-air.

CHRIS. So bad of me to defend you, was it?

DAVEY. I don't need your defence. Not like that.

CHRIS. I'll say nothing in future so.

DAVEY. Chris!

CHRIS *doesn't budge his eyes away from the TV screen.*

Do you know people barely look at me now? I never noticed it before if people looked at me but you notice it when they don't, like they'll catch something off your stare. I didn't do anything... And even if I did, which I didn't, do you deserve this? Do they deserve this? Them... I'm not saying they haven't done anything wrong, that they're not bad people but do they deserve the death penalty? Is that the best way to deal with them? Sometimes I just want to leave and go to Australia, Tanzania, somewhere far away from here. Where I can get on without everybody else's opinions. They weren't even there. I told you didn't I? That Mrs Gormley told my aunt she always knew I was doomed for badness because I knick-knacked her door when I was seven years old. Oh the warning signs were there alright if only we'd dealt with them sooner. Dealt with me how? How was I supposed to have been dealt with? How I'm being dealt with now?

CHRIS. You didn't do it, you'll be grand.

DAVEY. Doesn't matter whether I did or not. It's done now, this won't just go away.

CHRIS *turns from the TV and looks at* DAVEY *straight in the eye.*

CHRIS. But you didn't do it.

DAVEY. No, I didn't.

CHRIS. Then. It'll be fine.

CHRIS *goes back to the TV.*

DAVEY. I am grateful for everything you've done. Really, I am. I just quack quack quack quack HONK quack HONK quack quack.

CHRIS *turns to look at* DAVEY *again, perplexed.*

I just wished you'd told me about the radio thing before you went and did it. It's made everything impossible. They're even talking about the case in Dublin now.

CHRIS *ignores* DAVEY *and looks in a different direction.*

Chris...

SARAH *and her friend* ORLA, *who walks behind her, enter from the bar. They are carrying drinks.*

CHRIS (*to* DAVEY *and* SARAH). There's Sarah.

ORLA *walks out from behind* SARAH. CHRIS *stares at her. He sees* JANE.

(*To himself.*) Orla? (*To* ORLA.) Hi.

ORLA *doesn't respond. She stares at* CHRIS.

SARAH. What are you doing here?

CHRIS. Same thing you are I suppose.

SARAH. Are you stupid, or something?

CHRIS. I must be, yeah. Sit down anyway, while you're here.

SARAH *sits down opposite* CHRIS *and beside* DAVEY. ORLA *stands still. It's awkward.*

DAVEY. Hi, Sarah.

SARAH. Hi, Davey.

CHRIS (*to* ORLA). "Is everything okay?"

ORLA (*to* CHRIS). "Everything's fine. Can I have your phone number?"

SARAH. Sit down, Orla.

ORLA. No, thanks.

SARAH *stares at* ORLA.

DAVEY. How've you been? How's things?

SARAH. How do you think?

DAVEY. Much the same as myself, I'd imagine.

SARAH. I'd imagine you might be having a bit of a rougher time of it.

DAVEY. Maybe.

CHRIS. Why don't you sit down, Orla?

SARAH. Because she doesn't want to.

ORLA. I can speak for myself.

SARAH. Sorry.

ORLA. "I better go."

ORLA *stands still, staring at* CHRIS.

SARAH. You don't have to leave.

ORLA. Well I'm not sitting with them.

SARAH *rolls her eyes.*

I'm being unreasonable? I thought we were on a night out.

SARAH. We are.

ORLA. So, come on then.

SARAH. Where else are we going to sit?

ORLA. There's a group of them over there, see.

ORLA *points.*

SARAH. Don't point at them.

ORLA. Why wouldn't I, they're our friends?

SARAH. Just don't, okay. Don't draw attention.

ORLA. So you're not coming over then?

SARAH. Niamh is there. So is Claire.

ORLA. And?

SARAH. It'll be awkward.

ORLA. Awkward enough here.

SARAH. It doesn't have to be. Sit down. (*Lowering her voice.*)
I haven't seen you in weeks. I was looking forward to
tonight, please.

ORLA. So was I. But you didn't mention hanging out with…

ORLA *gestures at* DAVEY *and* CHRIS. DAVEY *looks
awkward.* CHRIS *is still struck.*

SARAH. We can move when another table becomes available.
Please?

ORLA. And have the girls not talking to me too?

SARAH. That's their problem.

ORLA. They are not the problem, Sarah.

SARAH. They've hardly been supportive.

ORLA. I think they've been pretty supportive.

ORLA *is referring to* JANE *and this dawns on* SARAH.

SARAH. Oh, okay. Supportive, just not of me then.

ORLA. This isn't about you.

SARAH. Of course it's about me, he's my brother.

ORLA. And you might be into blind loyalty but I'm not.

SARAH. 'Blind loyalty'?

ORLA. You keep defending them.

SARAH. 'Keep defending them'? We've only talked about
them once, Orla.

ORLA. Yes and why do you think that is?

SARAH. Oh right. So I'm supposed to just accept what she says
is that it? Do you even know the girl?

ORLA. No, do you?

SARAH. No but I know them, I've known them their whole
lives and they're fucking eejits but they're not criminals.

ORLA. Fair enough.

SARAH. No, not fair enough. I want you to understand what I'm saying and agree with me.

ORLA. I can't, Sarah. I just don't.

SARAH. So, what? I have to agree with *you* or else receive my marching orders? Just so you won't feel uncomfortable?

ORLA. Is that what you honestly believe?

SARAH. It's what you're saying isn't it?

ORLA. No, I'm saying that I've been in that girl's place before and so have you. Not raped not like that but not nothing either. I've been talked about like that. Sometimes to my face and again, so have you. And I know you love your brother. I thought he was a pretty good guy too but how you can look him in the eye when he's gone on public radio accusing that girl of going at herself with a chainsaw? What's going on with you?

SARAH. Orla…

ORLA. You've heard what your man on the radio said about the report from the sexual assault unit.

SARAH. Please.

ORLA. You heard it. Tell me you heard it. The tears in her –

SARAH *puts her hand up to stop*.

You just don't want to hear it.

Beat.

Okay. Stay here, enjoy your night. And I hope it all works out the way you want it to. But you'll realise, Sarah, eventually that "pricks like that, always get what's coming to them."

ORLA *leaves*. CHRIS *follows her until she has gone and then comes back to his seat*. DAVEY *goes to say something*.

SARAH. Don't! Please, just don't.

Pause.

DAVEY. Are you okay?

SARAH *recomposes herself.*

SARAH. Drink up, boys. I think we'd better be going home.

CHRIS. I'm going nowhere.

SARAH. I'm not leaving you here with them over there. Do you want another viral scandal on your hands?

CHRIS. Whose idea was it to go on the radio in the first place?

SARAH. I asked you to apologise. I didn't ask you to do whatever *that* was.

DAVEY. Pointless arguing it. It's done now.

SARAH. Easy for you to say.

DAVEY. No, it's not actually. It's made my life considerably worse too. And I understand why you asked him to do it but the rest of the country didn't give a bollix about the case until that interview. The Guards barely gave a shit. They'd forgotten it existed. But now that radio wanker is in contempt of court and we're front-page national news. So no, nothing's been easy on me, thank you.

SARAH. But the –

DAVEY. I know where this is going and I know you're upset and I'm sorry that your friends can't be more understanding but I am incredibly grateful to your brother and to you for standing behind me. And I'm sorry for all the grief it's caused you but you're the only people who are giving me the time of day.

SARAH. I'm sure there's a lot more than Chris batting for you.

DAVEY. What? Random middle-aged men in the street high-fiving me and telling me she was asking for it? Do you think that's the kind of support I want or need right now? Most of them believe it happened, they just don't believe it's a crime.

SARAH. There was a tear... the report.

DAVEY. A tear? A known crackpot, on a fourth-rate radio station, which he has since been fired from by the way, claims that he has read a report from a public hospital and you all assume to believe him without question. No follow-up, no nothing, no evidence that report even existed. He said it, so it must be true. Never mind the fact he's a known narcissist. None of this, none of anything of what has happened is based on fact. Just people listening and reading and assuming whatever suits them.

SARAH *is shook.* CHRIS *is glued again to the TV screen.*

Awkward pause.

SARAH. I'm sorry. I didn't mean to. I hadn't thought about it like that.

DAVEY. Whatever.

SARAH. No, I am. I can't imagine what that must feel like, for you.

DAVEY. I honestly don't care too much about what the general public has to say about it. Just really hurts when the people I care about do.

SARAH. I'm sorry.

DAVEY. I knew I shouldn't of come here.

DAVEY *gets up and turns to go.*

SARAH. I do believe you, you know. I don't know what happened but I know you, so.

DAVEY. Thank you.

DAVEY *leaves.* SARAH *looks on regretfully.*

CHRIS *jumps out of his chair.*

CHRIS. GOAL!!!!!!!!!!!

CHRIS *does a victory dance around* SARAH *and she leaves.* CHRIS *rearranges the set.*

Scene Six

One year later. A restaurant. CHRIS *sits alone. Waiters pass.*
MARIE *enters eventually. She is flustered and apologetic.*

MARIE. Oh my God. I am so *so* sorry.

CHRIS. It's fine, don't worry about it.

MARIE. Sorry.

　CHRIS *sees* JANE.

CHRIS. "No, I'm sorry, you just gave me a fright that's all."

　CHRIS *snaps out of it.*

MARIE. No it's not. It's not okay, I had it happen to me once.
First date…. Leaves me waiting outside for fifteen minutes
and then doesn't even acknowledge it when he arrives. Not
a dickie, as if I got it wrong, the time, but I've got the text
message, I've got the proof. But anyway yes, yes I'm so
sorry please forgive me.

CHRIS. Seriously, you're fine. So fine. You're not even that late.

MARIE. Just remember: Marie – not an asshole.

CHRIS. Marie – asshole, got it.

　Beat.

　I'm just messing…

MARIE. Oh sorry, yes, I got it, ha! I'm such an idiot, can't even
get a joke.

CHRIS. Seriously, you're grand.

　Awkward silence.

MARIE. Have you been on many of these then?

　Beat.

　Dates.

　Beat.

　Tinder, Bumble…?

CHRIS. Not really no.

Beat.

The odd one, maybe.

MARIE. Oh cool.

Beat.

I've been on a lot, like a lot. That makes me sound like a slut though doesn't it? That's not what I mean. I don't mean that I've slept with a lot of men, dates don't always mean sex, I mean obviously sometimes they do but not all the time but I'm not having sex all the time. Like, trust me it's been a *whiiiile* since I got laid, had sex, trust me, a while.

Beat.

I have had sex though. I have had it with a few people. I'm good at it even, I think. I mean I definitely know what I'm doing I mean.

CHRIS (*hesitantly*). Great.

MARIE. I'm sorry, I can't believe I've just said any of that. You must think I'm mental.

CHRIS. Look, these things are nerve-wracking situations. You're fine.

Beat.

MARIE. Hmmm.

CHRIS. What?

MARIE. Nothing, you just sound different.

CHRIS. Different to what? We've never even met before. Maybe we have. "I've an awful memory."

MARIE. No, of course we haven't. Sure I'm only in Galway a hot minute. You just sound different, from the messages, I mean.

CHRIS. Messages?

MARIE. On Bumble.

CHRIS. Oh right.

Beat.

Sorry about that.

MARIE. Nothing to be sorry about. Sure who sounds like themselves these days. God some of the lads I've talked to online. I've had them believing I'm a full-on dominatrix. Me? Sure I've never even had sex with the lights on.

CHRIS. Right.

CHRIS *tries again to get a waiter's attention and misses.*

Ah for…

MARIE. So what do you do, Chris?

CHRIS. I work for my dad, for the foreseeable anyway, we run a paint business, in a bit of dire straits at the moment but you know, we'll see.

MARIE. Paint?

CHRIS. Paint, yeah.

MARIE. That is so cool! Do you get to name the paints? I think I'd be really good at that actually, what kind of colours do you do?

CHRIS. Red, yellow, pink, green, purple, orange, blue. All the colours really. Mainly for industrial companies now but eh yeah, all the colours.

MARIE *thinks deeply.*

MARIE. Marshmallow Kisses for white or Makes the Boys Wink for pink, Midnight Embrace for black. What do you think, would you hire me?

CHRIS. I'd certainly consider it yes.

MARIE. Good. I'll call up Ronan Daly Jermyn, so. Tell them I've quit!

CHRIS. "You're an accountant so?"

MARIE. "No, no, just admin stuff, secretarial but they don't call it that any more."

CHRIS. Right...

MARIE. Did you always want to work in paint? Or the family business I mean?

CHRIS. I'm not sure really, I suppose it just made sense, easy way in and all.

MARIE. But it's not going well now?

CHRIS. Difficult to compete, competitors and stuff, bad PR for a while. Just a perfect storm for the moment.

MARIE. That must be tough.

CHRIS. It's fine, and yourself? What brought you to the west?

MARIE. I asked for a transfer to Galway last year. Dublin's a bit mad, too pressurised for me. I like that when I'm working here I don't feel too far away from anything else. It's not just a city. Does that make sense? Galway is smaller, more accessible and to be honest just a whole lot nicer. As a community I mean.

CHRIS *looks at her.*

Not a fan?

CHRIS. No, nothing like that. I love Galway, it's home, like. Just been a rough couple years. Community-wise.

MARIE. I probably have rose-tinted glasses. Newbie in town and all that. I'm sure Galway's not perfect.

CHRIS. Better than Dublin though!

MARIE. Haha! Yes. For definite.

CHRIS. Just some people giving it a bad name.

MARIE. Probably, sure you heard about those lads bragging about raping some poor girl over texts.

Silence.

CHRIS. They weren't bragging and he didn't rape her, he didn't even have sex with her.

Beat.

MARIE. Oh. Right.

Beat.

I haven't seen the messages. Someone in the office just told me about it. Apparently the trial is coming up soon.

CHRIS. Two months.

Beat.

MARIE. Friends of yours?

CHRIS. Yes.

MARIE. I'm sorry. I should've kept my mouth shut. Sure what do I know?

CHRIS. Yeah.

MARIE. I didn't mean to upset you.

CHRIS. You haven't.

Pause.

MARIE. How are your friends?

CHRIS. Tired.

MARIE *is trying to figure out whether she wants to leave.*

MARIE. It's a long while to be waiting to go to trial. Two years.

CHRIS *looks at her.*

I'm a legal secretary, Ronan Daly Jermyn. All criminal trials take two years.

CHRIS. I'm aware.

MARIE. Of course you are. No wonder they're tired.

CHRIS. We should be fine. There's not enough evidence to convict and she's lying so…

MARIE. Right. You…?

CHRIS. I was the one deleted the text messages.

MARIE. Okay. You weren't –

CHRIS. No, no. I saw her though, after her alleged 'rape'.

MARIE. You did?

CHRIS. Yep. She was fine. We had a few beers together and then she left. We think, the whole thing, it's all revenge on Davey. She thinks he took a photo of her with her boob out. He didn't.

MARIE. Revenge? I see.

MARIE *is awkward*.

CHRIS. You can leave if you want. I won't mind. I'm just not hiding this stuff, not when we haven't done anything wrong.

MARIE. I can respect that. Things aren't always as black and white as people want them to be.

CHRIS (*a brief relief*). Exactly.

MARIE. You seem certain though. That it didn't happen.

CHRIS. Well, again, I saw her. I was there.

MARIE *looks at the door again. She stops*.

MARIE. I was on a bus seven or eight years ago. I was on my way to work. It was the morning. I hadn't been feeling great. I think you've probably guessed by now that I'm a bit manic and if I wasn't selling myself before then, I really am now.

CHRIS. You're fine.

MARIE. Good, yeah... I'm a bit manic... some of the time and then the other of the time it's almost like I'm nothing at all, just kind of stagnant, just nothing. I flit between the two. I was down, this day on the bus. As in nothing. I was nothing.

CHRIS. Okay...?

MARIE. This man gets on the bus. He sits down opposite me. There is another man to the left of us, who is quite a bit older. The younger man asks the older one the time and he tells him. The younger man then follows this up with a comment about the weather and the older gent ignores him and shifts over in the seat. And I feel sorry for him, he seems

like me, like nothing, but at least he's trying, I'd barely
spoke a word in a week and at least he's trying to be seen.
I smile at him, so he's not as disheartened, that there's sound
people out there still, not to give up hope. He moves to face
me and I feel slightly uncomfortable, as in, I hadn't really
wanted to talk to him myself, just wanted him to know that
you could still if you wanted to, talk to strangers, it's not that
weird. But not me, right now, I didn't want to talk to anyone
but here he is in front of me and I am 'seen' I suppose… He
starts to touch at me anyway, my legs, as if to get my
attention, get me to respond to his now crazy questions about
coming away with him, escaping it all with him like he can
feel my sadness too, like I can feel his but why is he
grabbing at my legs as if it's part of the question? Sliding
them up until he's touching me. Touching me. He starts
licking his hands then and taking himself out of his trousers
and rubbing himself and I don't know what's happened but it
feels like it's my fault because I smiled at him. Nobody
around me is doing anything, just averting their eyes. One or
two of them move away, the old man does, goes right up the
front of the bus and I think maybe he'll tell the driver, but he
doesn't, just looks in the opposite direction. And the rest of
them, the passengers, are looking away from him too, from
me. They aren't asking him to stop, they aren't telling the
driver and I'm not sure what's happening but it feels wrong.
But if they're not reacting to it, can it be? Can it be wrong?
It mustn't be wrong, it's feeling like assault but nobody else
is responding to it in that way so it can't be, can it? And I sit
there quietly, him still at himself and me, until it's close
enough to my work that I can get off. Five stops early. And
he's blocking my exit but I get through eventually… And he
screams at me as I make my way to the top of the bus, about
having to put my hands in my knickers someday. And the
bus is quiet, looking at me, not him and I'm just…
unresponsive. And I walk to work and calmly go through my
day because I'm not sure what's just happened but it couldn't
have been assault. People don't like assault, they stop
assault, that couldn't have been assault.

CHRIS *is now looking at her straight on.*

So I want to know how you just know? How you feel so confident having seen her after the 'alleged'? When people don't even seem to know what assault is when it's happening there in front of them?

Pregnant silence.

A change in tone.

CHRIS. What do you want me to say?

Beat.

I said what do you want me to say, Marie.

A change in tone.

"I'm sorry that happened."

Beat.

MARIE. "What are you sorry for, Chris?"

Beat.

CHRIS. "I'm sorry that happened."

MARIE. "What are you sorry for, Chris? You didn't do it."

CHRIS *stands up, freaked out.*

CHRIS. What do you want me to do?

MARIE. I don't want you to do anything?

CHRIS. It's not my fault.

MARIE. I know that.

CHRIS. "I'm sorry that happened" to you.

MARIE. Thank you.

CHRIS. "Pricks like that always get what's coming to them."

CHRIS, *realising what he's said, shakes it out of him and looks at* MARIE.

MARIE. "Quack."

CHRIS. What?

MARIE. Nothing.

A waiter who has been watching is filming them on their phone. CHRIS *runs off desperately and watches* MARIE. *She begins to cry. She gets up and leaves the stage.* CHRIS *takes a moment and then gets up to rearrange the set solemnly.*

Scene Seven

Four months later. An area in the Galway Circuit Court House. ANDY, DAVEY *and* CHRIS *are dressed in suits.* ANDY *is sprawled out on a bench,* DAVEY *is pacing in the corner and* CHRIS *is sitting and slightly imitating* ANDY's *pose.*

ANDY. Okay what about... A dog or a donkey.

CHRIS. JESUS.

DAVEY. Andy, please.

ANDY. I'm sorry, David, but I've been sat here about two hours and I'm about to do my fucking nut in.

Beat.

CHRIS.... What kind of dog?

DAVEY. Well don't encourage him.

CHRIS. It's not like there's much else to be doing.

ANDY. Any dog you'd like, Chris.

DAVEY *looks at* CHRIS *as if to say 'don't'.* ANDY *looks at him encouragingly.*

A moment.

CHRIS. The dog.

ANDY. You sicko.

CHRIS. It's better than a fucking donkey.

ANDY. Right, my turn. Who am I riding and who am I sucking?

DAVEY. WILL YOU STOP PLEASE? If anyone hears you, I swear to God. It's like you're doing this deliberately.

ANDY. Oh calm down, man, Jesus. We've literally no worries here, it would want to take some leftist *nut-bag* of a Judge for us to end up anywhere but back home. Never mind she changed her story about fifteen times.

DAVEY. Great to hear you so confident, Andy.

CHRIS. He has a point to be fair, at one point she said I asked *her* for her phone number.

DAVEY. I don't think that's the gaping piece of evidence you seem to think it is.

CHRIS. Still, inconsistency. What was she even trying to suggest with that?

DAVEY. I doubt she was suggesting anything, just tripping over herself.

CHRIS. Like I'd ask a girl for her phone number after they've just banged my mate.

DAVEY. I didn't bang her.

CHRIS. Yeah but like I obviously thought you had at that time.

DAVEY. Obviously.

ANDY. They did find sperm on her though, didn't they? On her top. It was on that report from the sexual assault unit?

DAVEY. I said we didn't have sex, I never said I didn't ejaculate.

ANDY. Fair enough, I think most of them assumed you had sex anyway, it wasn't exactly taken as some big 'AHA!' moment in the whole thing wasn't it not?

DAVEY. No.

ANDY. Gas though really isn't it? Sergeant Nonce was right, some bint must have slipped him the report. You'd almost respect the fucking loser for whatever he did to get that.

DAVEY. Yeah, you should ask him round to the celebration gaff-party that your parents seem to have planned for you. Thank *Leo* for all he's done for us.

CHRIS. They said it was impossible to date the tears though, they could've occurred any time in the previous six months so, I can't say he was totally right in his presentation of it.

ANDY. Ah still it was all pretty gas. *Sergeant Nonce.* I mean that was a royal shitshow. It was some performance, Chris. Presenting yourself as some sort of axe-murderer. I was pissing myself laughing until I remembered that it was directly going to affect me.

CHRIS. Cheers.

ANDY. I mean between that and making some girl cry in a restaurant, you've literally become more well known in this trial than Davey for fuck's sake.

DAVEY. It was great for Chris to have your support throughout the whole thing anyway. So good of you to be there for him, and me too.

ANDY. I've been busy.

DAVEY. Making an ass out of yourself around town you mean?

ANDY *squares up to* DAVEY.

ANDY. And why shouldn't I?

CHRIS. At least you've had some fun. By the end of today, you might end up the brightest star of us all.

ANDY. What's that supposed to mean?

CHRIS. It means you're the DPP's strongest case.

ANDY. That's scaremongering.

CHRIS. You're the only one did what she said you did. You walked in, with your dick out.

ANDY. I was getting a condom.

CHRIS. It is what she said it is in the eyes of the law.

ANDY. You deleted the evidence.

CHRIS. It's not evidence if there was no crime.

ANDY. Fuck off…

This has slightly shaken ANDY.

They put me away for that and I'll never put my dick back in my trousers again. I'll be like that mattress girl but without the mattress.

Beat.

(*Thinking that no one has gotten the joke.*) Because my dick is the mattress.

DAVEY. Shut up, Andy.

SARAH *knocks on the door and stands in the doorway.*

SARAH. Is it okay if I…?

DAVEY. Come on in.

SARAH. Vibe in there is a bit weird.

DAVEY. It's a bit weird in here too.

SARAH. I can imagine.

CHRIS. Are Mam and Dad –

SARAH. They've gone for a coffee. The waiting was getting a little much. But I probably don't need to tell ye that. Dad's acting like he's on trial anyway the way he's going on.

DAVEY. A lot riding on it for him too I suppose and you and… everyone.

CHRIS (*to* DAVEY). A lot riding on it for you.

DAVEY. Obviously.

An awkward pause.

SARAH. Karen, my friend, knows her, Jane. Or knows of her, same estate. She paints an interesting picture of her anyway.

DAVEY. I really don't… it doesn't matter any more I suppose.

ANDY. What does she say?

SARAH. Just that she wouldn't be overly surprised by it being a lie. That if it was, 'revenge', like you said.

SARAH *indicates to* CHRIS, *who barely looks back.*

ANDY. Well we could've told you that two years ago.

SARAH. I heard there might be a precedent. She says she's a smart girl who's had a lot of problems growing up.

ANDY. It's not an excuse.

SARAH. I'm not saying it's an excuse just that her behaviour can be erratic and... she had a bad experience once and now she...

ANDY. A bad experience?

SARAH. She's been hurt, before. Of course it doesn't excuse what she's done. Taking revenge on someone for a photo that they never even took? It's hardly the work of a balanced person now is it?

ANDY *shoots* DAVEY *a slight look.*

CHRIS. Sarah.

SARAH. Just... poor girl, really.

ANDY. What do you mean 'poor girl'? She's not facing a jury.

SARAH. No, totally, I just mean, she's clearly disturbed, that's all.

ANDY. Well put her in a fucking loony bin then.

DAVEY. Andy, stop.

DAVEY *stands between* ANDY *and* SARAH. DAVEY *and* ANDY *stare each other down.*

SARAH. Look, can I get you guys anything? Coffees or water or burritos, even?

ANDY. I can get it myself.

SARAH. I know, but there's people gathering outside now with the verdict so near I just thought I'd offer in case you didn't –

ANDY. I can go wherever I want.

CHRIS. Could you get me a Fanta or something?

SARAH. Yeah of course.

DAVEY. A water would be great, Sarah. Thanks.

SARAH (*to* ANDY). Are you sure you don't want anything?

ANDY. I told you, I can get it my fucking self.

CHRIS. Don't talk to my sister like that.

ANDY. I'll talk to anyone whatever way I want.

CHRIS. She's just trying to help.

ANDY. Oh you and your family are so good at helping aren't you? Don't you dare start attacking my behaviour when you're the one that's gotten us into this fucking mess. Isn't that right, Padre Pio?

CHRIS. How is this my fault?

ANDY. Do you think the DPP would've given a fuck about this case if you hadn't've garnered us this much publicity?

CHRIS. Are you serious?

ANDY. I mean you've spent most of your life being some quiet shitty book boy I just never realised you were better off keeping your mouth shut. I swear to God you've been nothing but a fucking jackhammer since this thing started. It's like you want to send yourself to prison. If you don't like my behaviour then get out of the fucking house-party. If you can't stand back and fully admit that you have made this whole experience a hell of a lot worse for everyone involved then you're more delusional than I thought. You can't blame it on me when you're the one helping deny it ever happened. It's gotten to the point now where I fucking wish we *had* done what she said we did cos at least then I wouldn't feel like I'm completely being made a mug out of.

DAVEY. Andy.

ANDY. What?

CHRIS *looks at this exchange.*

Silence.

DAVEY. Get out.

ANDY. You get out.

DAVEY. Leave now.

ANDY. And go where?

DAVEY. Anywhere. You're the one says you can go anywhere you fucking want. Now get out. Go get yourself a Club Orange, just leave the rest of us and don't come back.

ANDY. Are you trying to tell me that this wouldn't have been a whole lot easier if dickwad hadn't blown his load live on air? If he hadn't made some girl cry in a restaurant warranting a bazillion Instagram posts? Do you know what allegiances you're picking here?

Beat.

What are you going to do next, show up at Jane Scully's front door with a bouquet of roses, say sorry and ask her to go out with you? You fucking clown.

CHRIS. You're a / clown

ANDY. Oh you can shut up, I've only been putting up with you the past fifteen years because of him, I don't give a shit what you have to say now.

CHRIS *cowers slightly.* SARAH *notices.*

DAVEY. Go outside to all your fans, have your little party, leave Chris alone and never talk to me again, ever. You can't polish a turd, Andrew.

SARAH. Davey, it's quite bad out there I don't –

DAVEY. He doesn't need your concern, Sarah, trust me, he has enough of his own.

ANDY *shrugs defensively. He very hesitantly opens the door and exits.*

CHRIS. He'll be on the warpath now.

DAVEY. Let him. I'm not sure there's much left to wage war on at this rate.

SARAH (*to* DAVEY). Are you okay?

DAVEY. I'm… I'm fine. Just happy to say goodbye to it whatever the outcome.

SARAH. For what it's worth I think you did the right thing.

SARAH *and* DAVEY *look at each other.* CHRIS *looks at them.*

DAVEY (*reluctantly*). Thanks.

SARAH *and* DAVEY *leave the stage.* CHRIS *tiredly begins to move the set around for the next scene.*

Scene Eight

Ten months later. The kitchen of MEGAMOUTH Insurance. CHRIS *enters.* ALEX *stands looking into a cupboard, his back towards* CHRIS. *He turns around.* CHRIS *sees* LEO. *The kettle is boiling.*

ALEX. "Christopher Christopherson! My man!"

CHRIS. Leo…

ALEX. Alex. You must be the new guy.

CHRIS. That would be me, yeah.

CHRIS *and* ALEX *shake hands.*

Beat.

ALEX. Hope you're finding everything alright, everyone's been nice, that kind of thing.

CHRIS. Oh yeah, they've been great, it's all great.

ALEX. Really? God, I must take it for granted so. I've been here about five years, easily done I suppose.

CHRIS. Five years, now that's commitment.

ALEX. Where did you come from yourself?

CHRIS. Oh, em, a paint company?

ALEX. Dulux, something like that?

CHRIS. No, it was, it was my family business actually.

ALEX. Had a fall-out with the old man was it?

CHRIS. Fall-out with the banks more like, it closed a couple of months ago.

ALEX. Sorry to hear that. Probably difficult to compete with Big Paint, those captains of industry.

CHRIS. Yeah, definitely.

ALEX. How did your family take it?

CHRIS. I mean, my dad was near retirement age anyway, so not amazingly badly. But my sister, she worked there too, I think she'd have designs on starting something else up. Hasn't had much luck finding anything new. But she's at the mercy of my dad really and I think he's having a bit too much fun on the couch for the moment.

ALEX. Was that all to do with the trial do you reckon?

CHRIS. What?

ALEX. Sorry, I, just when we saw someone new was starting, Carol recognised the name. Hard not to really, sorry, I shouldn't have said anything.

CHRIS. No, I suppose I should be used to it by now.

ALEX *looks at* CHRIS *like he has a million questions but can't think which one to ask first.*

ALEX. Tough old few years for you.

CHRIS. You could say that.

ALEX. How are the boys doing?

CHRIS. The boys?

ALEX. The other two.

CHRIS. Oh, Andy's gone to America and Davey's gone back studying I think.

ALEX. Studying? I hope it was a choice rather than a last resort. He's an innocent man, I'm sure they'd see him for a job in here if he wants it.

CHRIS. Solicitor exams, he has a traineeship. He's grand. I think, anyway. Haven't spoke to him much since the, whole, thing.

ALEX. I was delighted ye got off anyway. It's nice to see the justice system work for once.

The kettle is still boiling and the noise continues to heighten as the scene goes on.

CHRIS *looks at* ALEX, *mistrustful, as if he's having an out-of-body experience.*

You can't get away with doing that to people.

CHRIS *is deeply uncomfortable and doesn't respond. He regroups.*

CHRIS. What department do you work in, Alex?

ALEX. "Galway's third-most-listened-to radio station. Le-le-le-like a G6fm Galway's Premier Rockathon."

CHRIS *looks at* ALEX, *confused.*

CHRIS....

ALEX. I'm an accountant. I'm head of the accounts department.

CHRIS. Of course you are.

KATE *enters, stern.* CHRIS *sees* JANE.

ALEX. There she is.

KATE. Hi.

KATE looks at CHRIS as if to say 'move'.

CHRIS. Oh, sorry.

ALEX. I'm just teaching the newbie the ropes.

KATE. Very good.

ALEX. Have you two met yet?

CHRIS. "I'm sorry but what's your name again? I know I've met you before, I just, I've an awful memory."

CHRIS snaps out of it.

Chris, nice to meet you.

CHRIS offers a hand KATE doesn't take it.

ALEX. This is Kate. Head of the Social Committee this one.

CHRIS. Oh, really?

KATE. That's me.

ALEX. Planning a welcome party for you no doubt.

KATE snickers.

Some get-to-know-you drinks.

KATE. Oh I know him.

CHRIS. Have we met before?

KATE. I know you from around.

CHRIS. "Sorry, we could've been in school together for all I know, and I still would've forgotten."

CHRIS shakes it off.

KATE. We've been at the same parties. Me and your friends.

CHRIS gets what's going on.

CHRIS. Look, I don't want any grief.

KATE. And what? Because I won't smile at you and make niceties I'm giving you grief?

CHRIS. Fair enough.

ALEX. Will you give the lad a chance?

KATE. He's had a load of chances. He doesn't need one from me as well.

ALEX. He's an innocent man, Kate.

KATE. Oh yeah, innocent? Of what? I've been at those parties, I featured in that WhatsApp group.

CHRIS. I don't even know you?

KATE. I'm not talking about *your* WhatsApp group. I'm talking about the other one.

ALEX. "But you didn't delete that one. And why was that?"

CHRIS. Oh, right.

KATE. They probably told you it was just a bit of a laugh did they?

CHRIS *doesn't respond.*

Harmless fun?

CHRIS. "I'm sorry that happened."

KATE. "What are you sorry for, Chris. You didn't do it."

CHRIS. I don't know anything about the other one.

KATE. I think you'd have an idea, given how well you spoke in your own group.

CHRIS. It's not my group.

KATE. You do know your friend, David, took a photo of Jane at a party? Months before he raped her now, but yeah. Her boob had popped out. He thought he'd immortalise it in their little WhatsApp group.

CHRIS. "I don't think so."

KATE. He didn't tell you that?

ALEX. "Or did you delete that too?"

CHRIS. It wasn't him that took it. She got that wrong.

KATE. She got what wrong?

CHRIS. He didn't take the photo. He didn't know what she was talking about.

KATE. And I'm telling you now that he did know. Because I was there when he took the picture.

CHRIS. "I'm sorry that happened – "

KATE. "What are you sorry for, Chris?"

ALEX. "Let me lay this to you plain, Chris. You didn't rape the girl. I'm not angry at you, nobody's angry at you, okay?"

CHRIS. Fuck off.

ALEX. What?

KATE. Then he lied to you?

CHRIS. He didn't take the picture.

KATE. I saw him. Chris. I saw him take the picture.

CHRIS. No…

KATE. Well what's the other explanation?

CHRIS. He said he didn't know.

KATE. Well he did know.

ALEX. "Is that something he'd done before, penetrated an inanimate object?"

CHRIS. "I'm sorry that happened."

KATE. "What are you sorry for, Chris? You didn't do it."

CHRIS. He might have taken a picture but he didn't rape anyone. He didn't have sex with her.

KATE. But he's a liar. He lied to you. So how do you know he didn't?

The kettle is near the boil. We hear JANE *singing 'Friends in Low Places'.*

CHRIS. He didn't have sex with her.

KATE. How would you know, Chris?

CHRIS. Because I saw her.

KATE. You saw her do what?

CHRIS. She was fine.

KATE. "So I want to know how you just know? How you feel so confident having seen her after the 'alleged'? When people don't even seem to know what assault is when it's happening there in front of them?"

CHRIS. You weren't there.

KATE. But you were there were you? In the room with them? I was there when he took that photo.

ALEX. "Is that something you do often, you and your boys? Watch, is it? Getting off on the birds or each other?"

CHRIS. Stop.

KATE. "No, I'm saying that I've been in that girl's place before and so have you. Not raped not like that but not nothing either. I've been talked about like that. Sometimes to my face and again, so have you."

CHRIS. "I'm sorry that happened."

KATE. "What are you sorry for, Chris?"

CHRIS. I'm sorry.

KATE. "What are you sorry for, Chris?"

CHRIS. It doesn't mean he…

KATE. What does it mean, Chris?

CHRIS. It doesn't.

KATE. "We're friends now, aren't we?"

CHRIS. It doesn't mean he raped her. If anything it means it could've been definitely revenge.

KATE. What does it mean, Chris?

CHRIS. Revenge.

KATE. That's not what it means. What does it mean, Chris?

ALEX. What does it mean?

KATE. What does it mean about Davey, Chris?

Beat.

CHRIS. He's a liar…

KATE. Thank you.

> KATE *walks away and continues making her lunch. It is like nothing ever happened.*

ALEX. "You're not a bad guy, Chris, you never were but even you have to realise eventually, nine times out of ten, if it talks like a duck, it's a duck."

CHRIS (*quietly*). Quack.

> CHRIS *looks at* ALEX, *who looks back at him oddly. Everything is back to normal.* CHRIS *leaves defiantly and begins to change the set.*

Scene Nine

Later that day. DAVEY's *apartment.* CHRIS *bursts through the door as* DAVEY *opens it.*

DAVEY. Hello.

CHRIS. Hi.

> DAVEY *looks to a closed door behind him. The confidence* CHRIS *comes in with slowly begins to wane.*

DAVEY. Everything okay?

CHRIS. Why wouldn't it be?

DAVEY. I don't know, it's just been a while, that's all.

CHRIS. I'm sorry I haven't been in touch.

DAVEY. I think it's a bit more than that. You've been flat-out
ignoring my texts for one.

CHRIS. I've been busy.

DAVEY. Oh yeah, doing what?

CHRIS. New job and all that.

DAVEY. I heard, heard the new boss is a bit of a wanker too.

CHRIS. Bit of a clown, yeah.

DAVEY. A bit different when your dad's in charge maybe.

CHRIS. Definitely don't have that luxury this time, no.

Pause.

I wanted to…

DAVEY *looks back to the closed door again.*

DAVEY. You wanted to what?

CHRIS. Talk, I suppose. I've been thinking, a lot and –

DAVEY. And you miss me?

CHRIS *looks at him.*

CHRIS. I'm sorry, I haven't been in touch.

DAVEY. You and everyone else really. Getting proved innocent
doesn't seem to mean much to people.

CHRIS. That's not true. You had loads of support.

DAVEY. Really?

CHRIS. Yes.

DAVEY. Okay, well, if that's what you've come to say.

CHRIS. It's not.

Beat.

Have you heard from Andy?

DAVEY. No, should I have?

CHRIS. No, I was just…

DAVEY. Off with the Yanks.

CHRIS. A yanking good time.

DAVEY. Yeah.

CHRIS. How's the… the studying?

DAVEY. Good, yeah. Nice being paid to read.

Pause.

CHRIS. Davey… could I've a cup of tea or something?

DAVEY. What?

CHRIS. A coffee or.

DAVEY looks to the closed door again.

DAVEY. Sorry, no milk.

CHRIS. Alright.

Pause.

DAVEY. What do you want, Chris?

CHRIS. I'm here because you…

CHRIS looks at DAVEY.

You.

The door behind DAVEY slowly squeaks open. SARAH stands there.

SARAH. Chris…

CHRIS stares at SARAH in disbelief.

Hi.

CHRIS. Hi?

DAVEY and SARAH look to each other.

A pregnant silence.

SARAH. Hi Chris?

CHRIS. What the fuck are you doing here, Sarah?

SARAH. Listen, I know this probably looks strange.

CHRIS. Yeah, it looks really fucking strange.

SARAH. I'm sure it does. I'm sorry that we didn't get a chance to tell you properly, what was happening.

CHRIS. What's happening?

SARAH. Chris. I wanted to make sure that it, well we both wanted to make sure that it was serious before we told you. Davey's been trying to contact you the past while. We've both been trying to –

CHRIS. Are you taking the piss?

SARAH. Chris, please.

CHRIS. You and him?

DAVEY. My name is Davey.

CHRIS. Your name is David. Now shut up.

SARAH. Don't speak to him like that.

CHRIS. I'll speak to him whatever way I want.

DAVEY *stares at* CHRIS *very intensely.*

SARAH. I get that we've caught you off-guard, okay. But this wasn't planned. We just started talking, texting each other and one thing led to… you know what I mean.

CHRIS. Stop.

SARAH. I had no one else to talk to.

CHRIS. You had me!

SARAH. I've barely seen you, you're barely home. You can't look Dad in the eye and you certainly haven't exactly asked me how I am, Chris.

CHRIS. But he has, has he?

SARAH. Yes, he has. He's done a lot more than that.

DAVEY. I love her, Chris.

SARAH. What's wrong with you? What's wrong with this?

CHRIS. You're my sister.

SARAH. And?

CHRIS. And he's... he's...

DAVEY. I'm what, Chris?

Pause.

CHRIS. You're... my friend.

SARAH. Your friend? We're not fifteen any more. I'm allowed go out with your friends.

CHRIS. Yeah but not...

SARAH. ...

CHRIS. I didn't see it.

SARAH. You didn't see what?

CHRIS. I didn't see it.

SARAH. Were you supposed to?

CHRIS. I mean, I didn't see it coming.

SARAH. I didn't know how you'd react.

CHRIS. And how did you think I'd react?

SARAH. Angry.

CHRIS. And why do you think that is, Sarah?

SARAH. I don't know, Chris, why is it?

Beat.

This is the only... the best thing to happen me in a long time.

SARAH *looks to* CHRIS, *who looks to* DAVEY. CHRIS, *defeated, makes a decision.*

CHRIS. You had to pick one of my friends, did you?

SARAH. At least you still have some.

CHRIS. I feel like a mug.

SARAH. Well you're not.

CHRIS. "I wasn't there when it happened."

SARAH. You're not supposed to be there when it happens, Chris. It's none of your business.

CHRIS. "I wasn't there when it happened."

SARAH. Why would you be? Do you think I want a chaperone on dates?

SARAH is caught up in CHRIS's words, but DAVEY knows exactly what he's saying. CHRIS looks to DAVEY and DAVEY looks to CHRIS.

I want you to be happy for me, for us. This is a good thing, Chris. A good thing that's come out of an awful situation. I want you to see that. It's something positive out of something negative. Can you see?

Beat.

CHRIS. I can see that yeah.

SARAH. We're happy.

SARAH stares at CHRIS, who avoids her gaze.

I'm going to get changed. We can talk about this on the way home.

DAVEY. I thought we were going for –

SARAH. No, I'm going to go home.

SARAH exits.

The tension is palpable.

Silence.

DAVEY. She didn't want to upset you. We weren't sure what was… She text me after that night, the one with Orla and…

CHRIS.…

DAVEY. It was just friendly in the beginning. I didn't plan on...

CHRIS....

DAVEY. She's been very good to me.

CHRIS....

DAVEY. I won't apologise for it.

CHRIS....apologise?

DAVEY. Is there something you want to say?

CHRIS....

DAVEY. You said that's why you were here.

CHRIS....

DAVEY. Talk.

Beat.

CHRIS....I didn't see it.

DAVEY. I didn't know how to tell you.

CHRIS. I didn't see it.

DAVEY. How do you tell your friend you've started seeing their sister?

CHRIS. I didn't see it.

DAVEY. Again, Chris, I don't know why you feel you should have.

CHRIS. Can't believe what I haven't seen, I suppose.

DAVEY. Can't you not?

They square up to each other slightly.

SARAH *re-enters. She looks at them cautiously.*

SARAH. Is everything okay in here? It's very quiet.

Silence.

This is something good, Chris. Please...

CHRIS. It's none of my business.

SARAH. No. I'll just get my bag and we'll go, we can talk about it on the way home.

SARAH *exits to the bedroom.* DAVEY *goes to follow her.*

CHRIS *goes to speak and* DAVEY *stops and looks at him.* CHRIS *says nothing.* DAVEY *exits.*

CHRIS *sits down in the couch and closes his eyes,* JANE *enters from the door* DAVEY *has just exited from.* JANE *goes to speak as* CHRIS *reopens his eyes. Blackout.*

A Nick Hern Book

Duck Duck Goose first published in Great Britain in 2021 as a paperback original by Nick Hern Books Limited, The Glasshouse, 49a Goldhawk Road, London W12 8QP, in association with Fishamble Theatre Company

Duck Duck Goose copyright © 2021 Caitriona Daly

Caitriona Daly has asserted her right to be identified as the author of this work

Cover image by Leo Byrne and Publicis

Designed and typeset by Nick Hern Books, London
Printed in Great Britain by Mimeo Ltd, Huntingdon, Cambridgeshire PE29 6XX

A CIP catalogue record for this book is available from the British Library

ISBN   978 1 84842 961 1

www.nickhernbooks.co.uk

facebook.com/nickhernbooks

twitter.com/nickhernbooks